1

Sex Begins In the Kitchen

A Marriage Manual for Men

Joe Hill

2

This book is dedicated to the
Love of my Life.

We took our eyes off the big picture

And let it slip away.

She knows who she is.

Introduction

One might expect that the author of this book has a wildly successful marriage with a wife who is the benefactor of a wealth of applicable marriage advice and knowledge, one who is still in love with the prince of her dreams. Oh, what I would give for that to be the case, but nothing could be further from reality. The truth is I am divorced from two wives spanning a total time-period of over thirty-six years and currently writing this book as an unmarried man who regrets losing the love of his life very recently, a man still feeling the pain of losing his best friend and the haunts that torment him over things he should have done before it was too late.

Many books are available on the subject of marriage authored by various experts with PhD's, Marriage and Family Counselors, Clergy and other relationship professionals who can boast of such long term successful marriages backed by much study and research. In many ways I envy them. However, if I have learned anything in my life of successes and failures it's that you can learn more from someone who has experienced failures and disappointments and the challenge of recovery first-hand. In the successful Alcoholics Anonymous program recovering addicts who truly wish to gain sobriety are not paired up with a person who has never had a drink or experienced drunkenness. Instead they are teamed up with a sober sponsor who has been there, traveled the same path and experienced the same downward spiral of alcohol dependency, so that the sponsor can recognize the signs associated with falling off the wagon, share words of encouragement from an empathetic perspective and offer some real "me too" support.

If you were thinking, or hoping this book is all about sex, it isn't, and yet it is. If you were hoping for a How To book involving sexual techniques on how to drive your woman wild in bed, subscribe to Cosmopolitan or get your own copy of Sex for Dummies. Rather my attempt with this book is to show that sex isn't as much about an ultimate climatic act as it is about everyday intimacy and the ways we can keep our wives interested and invested in our relationship. Carrying on a conversation and listening can be sexy to a woman. Cooking her dinner instead of waiting for her to cook yours can be sexy. Knowing how to work that vacuum on a Saturday morning can be sexy. Appreciating the bliss of simple quiet shared moments when words aren't needed can be sexy. All these things add to the expectation and the anticipation of all men know to be sex, but that women need, appreciate and respond to continually. If you ignore your wife but expect her to be turned on come the weekend, you are living in a man cave and need to read this book. Do it right and you won't be able to beat her off you when it is time for all that you define as sex. And while the chapter in this book regarding sex may indeed be the longest of the chapters by far because of the extreme importance the role of a fulfilled sex life plays in a successful marriage, it is my intent to show that these loving ways to show your wife your complete love and adoration outside of the coital act itself, in fact falls under the all-encompassing umbrella of intimacy.

It is with this in mind that I wanted to write this book while the scars are still healing and the pain of loss still stings. Men tend to get a false reputation of being hard, calloused and emotionally detached when it comes to relationships, but I know how wrong that perception can be. When we meet and fall for that special lady and build a life around her but end up losing her because we didn't handle our business as we should have as engaging husbands in order to preserve the relationship, we can end up just as emotionally distraught and messed up as any female counterpart. What we allow to show on the outside is generally not indicative of what we are feeling on the inside. We hurt just like anybody else when we are rejected, tossed aside and left behind. Contrary to the popular book written years ago, men and women are not from different planets, but perhaps just different sides of the same planet.

Many times a divorce is a result of acts we could not foresee or control and we are blindsided by the unexpected termination of our marriage. But many are the times when we either don't recognize or simply ignored the warning signs of a marriage in trouble, thinking it will somehow work itself out if we just give it time. And for others, there is just simply a lack of knowledge or desire to learn the skills required to please a woman for a lifetime. And by the time we may sense something is not right in the marriage, it may already be terminal with no cure.

The traditional vows that many couples still cite, "'*til death do us part*", is key to the longevity of a successful marriage. It's not as much a commitment to time, as some may interpret, but a commitment to remaining a loving partner through all the winds of individual change. When I turned thirty years old, I was not the same man I was at twenty. The same could be said when I turned forty and then fifty years old. As humans we are continually evolving, perhaps some more drastically than others, but changing nonetheless. Two people who commit to marriage in their twenties or thirties will be much different people in their forties and fifties due to circumstances, increased experience, life-changing events, weathered storms, etc. Loving until parted by death is a vow to recognize and accept those changes and being deliberate in continuing to love through the evolutionary process. For some that is a difficult proposition. When you lose sight of the person you married because you become obsessed with the more recent version of that person who is now before you, your marriage is doomed. A wise Proverb tells us to "love the wife of our youth", that is at all times remember the person who you fell in love with at the very beginning and let nothing in the future distract you from seeing him or her in the same loving way throughout the years of marriage. Value that relationship as if it were a priceless jewel and protect it at all costs. The alternative, a failed marriage and a broken heart and spirit is too high of a price to be paid. Trust me on this.

There is little worse than spending a large portion of your life building a family unit only to see it implode due to divorce. There is nothing as lonely and isolating than spending holidays alone when you once spent them surrounded by family. And there's not much that's more painful than photos posted on various social media platforms of families getting together while you sit at home with a television, completely abandoned, feeling the helplessness of being suddenly left out of events in which you were always included in years past. It is a pain I would not wish on any other man, a hole and a void seemingly impossible to fill. It is intensified by the knowledge that just maybe, you could have done things to change the outcome had you fully known the severity of the situation, but through either complacency or ignorance, you didn't. To know you could have changed things but didn't, is to suffer a personal hell.

If I can teach someone who reads this book how to save their marriage, how to step up and be the protective prince our ladies deserve and desire, and how to keep your woman falling in love with you continually over a span of decades, I will have accomplished something truly noble in my meager existence. I may or may not get the opportunity to apply these principles I've learned in my own future relationships-only God knows if there will ever be another Mrs., but if I ever do, watch out! Therefore, until that time comes, please accept my heartfelt advice and sincere wish to offer something of real, applicable value from someone who has been there, has failed but has learned what worked and what didn't. A famous singer back in the day had a hit called *If You Want to be Happy for the Rest of Your Life, Fall in Love With Your Wife*. It is my deepest desire that something in this short book may help someone do just that!

Love is a single soul
inhabiting two bodies

~Aristotle

As soon go kindle fire
with snow, as seek to
quench the fire of love
with words.

~ William Shakespeare

CONTENTS

10

A DOZEN LONG STEMMED ROSES

I sent my special lady

Just to let her know I cared

A dozen long stemmed roses

To express the love we shared

I hoped they'd last forever

They were all I had to give

And for her I'd make all efforts

To assure that they would live

The flowers looked so sturdy

Poised in elegance and grace

That I failed to see the water

Near the bottom of the vase

The next day started sadly

There revealed in morning's light

The remnants of a flower

That had perished in the night

A seed was all I gathered

While the rest was swept away

Making haste I added water

So no others would decay

One day I saw a blemish

Not severe, but yet I tried

To repair the tainted petal

But in vail the flower died

One by one the roses wilted

From my lack to meet their needs

Til a dozen long stemmed roses

Were reduced to scattered seeds

In spite of good intentions

Sometimes real but some for show

I neglected their attention

Just content to watch them grow

13

With nothing now but memories

If there's any solace found

It's a tiny bag of seedlings

I keep close where'er I'm bound

With the hope that maybe someday

Should fate become my friend

And bestow an opportunity

To replant the seeds again

But this time vow to nourish

So to cause to bloom once more

A dozen long stemmed roses

Shared with love like those before

Joe Hill, 1994

1. Dating Doesn't End With "I Do"

For some men, "I Do" quickly becomes "I Did" as if somehow the vows end the process of the chase; you made the basket, you rung the bell with the hammer, you knocked over all the bottles and now you can claim your carnival prize. Like a trophy won after a successful season, your wife becomes a trophy wife, a symbol of something you did instead of something you are just beginning. You should trade your trophy mentality for a Lifetime Achievement mentality because marriage isn't a sprint but rather a marathon. If you truly feel "I Do" represents the culmination of your courtship, you will be presented with immediate challenges in your young marriage.

You've spent enough time with this remarkable woman to know that if you're ever going to do it, or in some cases, be brave enough to do it again, she's the one. Plans have been made, credit cards maxed out and finally the big day arrives, that day when the two become one-and life gets real! Marriage is not the claiming of the prize-it is the beginning of the race to keep your prize. And it's the dating process that convinced you to enter the race.

Why is it so important to continue dating your wife long after the wedding vows have been cited and the honeymoon has come and gone? It's quite simple really. It is through dating that you most likely discovered that you loved this woman so much so that you decided to spend and share your life with her every day. It is through the courting process that the two of you learned all you needed to know about the other, the traits you found irresistible, the important things you shared in common, the annoying habits you dismissed for the greater reward, the potential compatibility of companionship and the contentment of commitment. If you were like me, once you discovered you possessed feelings for this special lady you could not wait to be with her again, and found that moments spent apart seemed like an eternity. The heart recognized something it had longed for and knew now that it would never beat the same without her to the point that separation seemed more like an illness with the only cure being reunion. You've been there, you know it to be true. Separation is the only illness for which there should never be a cure!

I was compelled to be creative in planning nights out with my new girlfriend. You always have the obvious options of dinner and a movie, but taking the time to learn what she liked presented opportunities to respond with activities and dates that she would remember. To you it may not have mattered what you did just so long as you were with her, but you were aware that you needed to woo her and romance her in ways that would get her to respond to you favorably and get her thinking about long term possibilities. Each date was exciting because it was planned ahead of time and it created anticipation for both parties that culminated in that eventual reunion, the date. You went dancing, you maybe even sang to her-you did things outside of your comfort zone in a state of ultimate vulnerability because people in love do crazy things without much thought of what onlookers may be thinking. You strutted your stuff to the fullest.

...and then you got married, and probably lazy.

It's not that you didn't still find her as desirable as you did before. It's just that the chase, the conquest ended-you won her-she's now your wife-you can stop trying so hard because she now shares your last name. After all, she just promised to love you whether sick, healthy, rich, poor, happy or unhappy-the legal and religious marriage cage. The notion that courting is no longer necessary after a wedding is a misconception that we men adopt too often. It can actually be the very first nail in the coffin of unfulfillment if we don't recognize it and take action to prevent it.

There are so many reasons for and benefits found in continual dating that books have been written dedicated solely to the subject. Ask any married woman and she can cite a memorized list of reasons to keep dating her. I'm sure most men understand the importance of maintaining at least some effort to have date nights. But setting up a home, combining incomes, the rigors of the respective jobs or careers, the physical fatigue associated with the normal work week-all contribute to letting something so important as dating fall by the side of the road. But men, these dates are so important! Just as women want to feel they are still the object of your desire and affection, truth be told, we feel much the same way. We need to know that our women still get hot and bothered when we're around and at our best-we need to have the affirmation that we are the man of her dreams, even on ordinary days of predictable work and domestic habits and routine. Men and women are alike in needing to be constantly reminded that our partner loves and wants us. Dating provides both men and women that opportunity. I can't possibly list all the reason to date your wife after the vows are recorded, but I will try to address just a few in this relative short chapter.

First, dating maintains an element of mystery.

One of the fun things about the first few dates was unveiling the mystery behind this lady who suddenly captured your attention. While the exposure of this mystery was important in determining if she was marriage material, the process of discovery was exciting. And it was just as much so for her! Marriage should never become so complacent that the quest becomes irrelevant. Women still want to be pursued by their mystery man, even by those who have already captured them. It rekindles fond memories of the initial chase. There are moments during your dates that each of you will never forget-the first time you held her hand, the first dance (men, learn to dance if you don't know how). There was the very first time you kissed-even if awkward, women remember these things. Men will remember the first time they slipped their hand under the blouse and women will recall his first touch-sparks! These are magical moments that don't have to be encapsulated as mere memories but can be reenacted on dates after marriage.

Second, dating reminds you of all the things that you saw in her that made you want to spend your life with her.

Women tend to be much more sentimental than their male counterparts and they can remember the smallest of details-that can be both a good and bad thing. Most women can recall each date, what they wore, where you took her, what you did, etc. The dates meant a lot to her and she enjoys the opportunity to relive them with you. Men need to be reminded of those nights and those moments when you begin to realize there may be something here. But dating also allows her the opportunity to recall all the qualities she was attracted to when she realized you were her Knight.

19

While those things can be displayed every day, dating focuses on the moments that started it all-nothing but good can come from reliving the first few dates when it was just the two of you and nothing else mattered.

Third-Children!

Yes, we love them-they are God's blessings to us and the ultimate result of two people who want to create a living being that represent the best of each parent. And some date nights need to include your children, especially if they are older. But too often after children enter the family picture, the couple loses their identities in the day to day responsibility of raising them and caring for them. And men, if you are blessed with a wife who feels called to be a stay-at-home mother, it is imperative to her sanity that you make every effort to get her out of the house on a regular basis, sans children, so that *a)* she can catch her breath and take a break from the noble but overwhelming task of full-time motherhood, and *b)* so she doesn't forget that you still find her as desirable as ever for the beautiful woman she is, the one you courted and married. If you really want to do it properly, plan a weekend away every three or four months and make it known so she can be looking forward to that time when it can be just the two of you for a brief few days.

Fourth, dating outside of the house in some neutral location gives ample opportunity to have healthy conversation.

We will discuss this more later in a chapter on the subject, but sometimes it's easier to be open and frank over a cup of Starbucks or a glass of wine. Whether she works every day in the home or outside of the home she probably misses discussions with you. Dates away from the TV or computer lets her know she has your total attention. Conversation and a listening ear are vital to a healthy marriage. This is the one area most men fall short. I know I did. If there are too many distractions in the home to facilitate quality time together, it is good on occasion to get out of the home, even if just for a walk in the evening air.

Fifth and last-it can lead to some passionate intimacy!

When you are dating you may or may not have had boundaries, especially in the early stage of courtship. You may have wanted to crawl all over her but agreed mutually to abstain for a period. She may have been reluctant to surrender herself completely to you without knowing for sure if you were the one or not. Now that you are a couple and the gloves are off, the boundaries lifted, only your imagination limits where the night and the date will end. MIND YOU, SEX SHOULD NOT BE THE OBJECTIVE OF THE DATE! If in fact it is, you have wasted precious moments with your bride that you can't recapture and that she needs from you. But if you shower her with affection and attention as the only object of your desire, the reciprocation might just be mind-blowing!

Date nights can be fun, active, romantic or laid back. If you don't know which approach to take, here's a hint-just do what she would prefer to do! And if you truly don't know, give some slips of paper and ask her to write down dates she would find exciting or meaningful, and then, every so often, just pick one-that way you can't go wrong. It will pay enormous dividends later. Be creative. Plan on picking her up at a certain time as if you weren't living with her, and show up with flowers. If money allows, show up in a limo and make a night of it. Your date could be entirely limited to the privacy of the limo (and the discretion of a well-tipped driver). Take her to a karaoke bar and sing her a love song. Plan a picnic with a bottle of wine and her favorite cheese or chocolates. Go get a massage together or, dare I suggest, a double pedicure. If you want to really ignite a spark, take her back to that place where you were first intimate! It might have been a hotel room, the front seat of your car, the barn down the road-be adventurous in ways that will cause her to remember. Surprise her with tickets to her favorite show or a concert. Try to impress her every bit as much as you did when you were still courting her before the marriage proposal. And on occasion, let her plan the date-just don't make a habit of it. Putting pressure on her to come up with the evening itinerary takes all the fun away from the process for her.

The number one all-important objective of continuing to date your wife is simply spending time together. While there may be a plethora of things you can do under the guise of a date, it's not as important how much money you spend on the date or how much you can pack into an evening out-in fact the best dates will be those that are not so packed with activities that it doesn't allow time for intimate conversation. Dates should be about the moments the two of you share together, the time invested in each other, the laying aside of all daily distractions to remember that which is most important, the marriage relationship and the stoking of the flame so that the heat of passion and love never goes out. Treat that fire like it's in danger of the elements of wind and rain-protect it from being extinguished by adding all the necessary fuel to feed the flames. The moment you take her love for granted and stop doing all that is required to keep your relationship alive and exciting and fresh, the moment you allow the possibility of someone else stealing your fire and taking over your campsite. Dating is your opportunity to protect and treasure your gem, your wife.

Whatever you end up doing, wherever you go, which ever approach, let the objective be your obvious love and continued attraction to her-make her feel like the school girl going to the Prom or the Princess in her carriage to meet her prince. Don't ever stop trying to win her affection, whether you're still newlyweds or just coming off your Silver Anniversary. She needs to know you will always see her as the girl you dated, chased and fell for.

2. Security in a Haunted House

Men, google any research on the subject or question any women you may know and they will tell you that they want security, stability and comfort in their marriage. But don't believe it for one moment, or at least don't believe that's all they want! Yes, your wife wants to know they are protected and safe, that you offer comfort and stability and that you are faithful to the marriage-these are important elements to a woman's need. Faithfulness, trust and protection in a relationship can't be overstated. However, if your home life is stable, predictable and overtly familiar, she will quickly get bored and restless. Familiarity in a marriage breeds boredom, and boredom in a relationship for both men and women can be a gateway to resentment and for some, infidelity. Regardless of what woman may say, they don't always want the same thing in the same way all the time. They like their comfortable flats for everyday chores, but on occasion they want to slip into their sexy stilettos and do the town. And if you think women just want the ho-hum static life where everything is easy and predictable, just take a look at the shoe closet.

Each October production companies spend millions of dollars in an attempt to create haunted houses that exceed the fright factor of the previous year. Scores of people young and old will buy their ticket and stand in line just to get the

24

holy feces scared out of them as they venture slowly and cautiously through the dark maze of the ghostly manor knowing that the next turn or room will hold some ghastly surprise that will cause their heart to jump a beat and their blood pressure to rise a few points over normal. Haunted houses are getting more creative and pushing the envelope more each year in order to remain relevant in the industry. What used to be poor actors dressed in innocent costumes are now paid professionals with real chainsaws. What were once dark rooms are now low-voltage mazes that you must feel your way out of at the risk of being shocked. If you are like my sons one house or production won't do the trick-you will visit as many as possible and compare the scare sensors and then tell your friends which house offer the most unique and thrilling experiences.

I used to wonder what it was that would cause sane people to be scared out of their shorts during the month of October. It's not only the haunted houses but the slew of horror movies that we will sit and watch that hardly catch our attention any other time during the year. I think I figured it out and it should serve you well if you view it in light of marriage. At least it's my untrained theory.

When we are first newlyweds it seems like the least little thing we do together is new and exciting because we have no real history as a couple-something new and unexpected at every turn. As we settle into domestication, we become *familiar* with each other and the daily routine. While perhaps still enjoyable, it becomes predictable and comfortable, like a favorite pair of everyday shoes. One of the biggest challenges any married couple faces is keeping the freshness and excitement alive after you've been

25

together for a few years. Successful marriages are those who recognize this syndrome and work hard to avoid the pitfalls of boredom. Haunted houses are thrilling because each and every turn brings an element of the unknown. We embrace it because we know in our intellect that the chainsaws are harmless, the blood is chemically reproduced, the spirits are just local actors and there is an eventual exit that takes us back to safety. And yet we love the momentary shock and the adventure of not knowing what's coming because we yearn for adventure in a safe and controlled environment.

This is precisely what our wives desire from us and the home life we help to create. While every day can't be a haunted adventure, men need to be just as creative in providing their mates elements of surprise, moments of the unknown, and most certainly anything that breaks the monotony of the daily domestic routine, a marital fun house if you will. You don't have to be a creative genius or put a lot of thought and planning into something new every day, but the TV and your sofa are not always your best friends if you want a happy wife and marriage. Sometimes you need to pull out the shock and awe elements to keep her on her toes.

This is a lesson I too should have learned much earlier. In hindsight I could have been proactive in reducing the familiarity factor. When both husband and wife work outside of the home and return in the evening, it is just too easy to sit in silence and watched preprogrammed television shows before heading to the bedroom just to start the process all over the next day. So, I want to list a few things that you can easily plan and put into play that will go a long way in eliminating boredom. These suggestions are particularly with your domestic life in mind and should not be considered as a substitute for your date nights, which we discussed in the previous chapter. And they certainly don't need to be implemented every single night, but mix it up for your wife and keep her at some level of anticipation, just like that haunted house. Ready, grab a pen.

1. *Get up thirty minutes early and have coffee with your wife on the porch or patio-NO NEWSPAPER!*

This is a great way to start some days and it allows your wife to know that spending the first few moments of the day with her is important to you! Take it a step further on the weekends and make her breakfast outdoors or in bed. Don't just serve her, stay with her-it is time well invested that will pay dividends long term.

2. *Tackle a new recipe together and make it fun.*

Don't be afraid to make a mess in the kitchen. You are never too old for a good old-fashioned food fight and flour in just the right spots can be a turn on for you both. Bake a cake and have fun spreading the icing. Take turns licking the bowl, or if it leads to it, each other. Sex really can begin, and sometimes climax in the kitchen. Have a backup dinner plan in case the recipe turns out less than scrumptious.

3. *Along the same line of thought, have an in-home picnic.*

Spread out a blanket in the family room and pop open a bottle of wine with some light food fare like cheese, crackers, fruit-finger foods so there in no cleanup required. Go with music instead of a TV. Nothing says I love you like a man who would rather watch the game than feed his spouse. Again, it's all about spending precious moments with her in a way that convinces her that you desire her more than anything else.

4. Play games!

Board games, card games, truth or dare games, some clothing ante strip poker-just make it fun. If you are daring, there are adult games available for purchase made exclusively for couples. Fun and games knows no age limit.

5. Plan a candlelight bath together.

Have some soft music, burn a scented candle, share some wine or her preferred beverage and just soak (pun intended) in the moment with no expectation, objective or agenda. If you are fortunate enough to have a private jacuzzi take it outdoors but incorporate the same elements. Be attentive-caress her feet, especially if she works outside of the home. Let her sit close without an octopus response. If she wants more you will know it. When finished, dry her off, rub her down with some nice body lotion and rinse the tub so she won't have to, as if it were a premarital date!

6. Plan a weekend nudity day!

If you can't be naked in front of your spouse, then who? Why not have some fun with it. This would be a day when you have no plans outside of the home and are not expecting any company or church folk! It is simply a day when you just go about your usual weekend domestic affairs, clothing optional. Have your breakfast naked, just watch the hot coffee. Run the vacuum naked. Watch a movie together naked. If you really want to give her the haunted house effect, the shock factor, just show up in the kitchen nude and tell her you will be that way for the balance of the day and invite her to join in. I can guarantee, she won't be bored that day. Laughing or even in hysterics, possibly, but not bored.

7. Rearrange the furniture together.

Men your home might be your castle, but your queen rules the roost. If like me, you may or may not have had any input into the selection of your furnishings or décor. But even if everything was chosen and placed by your wife, it can be a drag seeing the same things in the same position every day. So why not have some fun with it. It's amazing what a coat of new paint or a rearranged room can do to break up the monotony of a room that hasn't changed in several years. Take her lead, but try different settings to capture at least the appearance of a new room.

8. Buy a How To dance video and cut a rug.

Nothing shows a wife more vulnerability than a man with two left feet attempting to learn a few dance moves with or for his wife. I love to dance but never learned anything new and whenever we would go to the club she would make a point that I just did the same move over and over. In fact, we would be envious of couples who floated across the dance floor like Astaire and Rogers. So, buy or download dance instructions based on your preferred genre and boogie down together. It's not only a fun domestic activity but something that will make your date nights even more enjoyable. NEVER stop dancing together!

9. Have friends over for dinner or cocktails.

Some of our most enjoyable moments were those spent with other couples in the comfort of our home. Something amazing happens when good friends get together-they laugh! If there is anything I could go back and change in my failed marriage it would be to find more opportunities just to laugh. It's great to have close friends who enjoy your company in your home. I am convinced that the home is a living entity and that laughter and the positive effects linger long after the laughter dies down. There are moments for romance and gentleness, but there needs to be the same moments for brevity and joy.

10. Have regular family gatherings or cookouts.

For many of the same reasons mentioned above, moments and memories are created when family gets together whether for special occasions or just for a weekend barbecue. If your extended family is in close proximity to your home, they need to be frequent fixtures and feel welcomed to visit their second home. It is these gatherings that we learn the details of how their lives are going, especially important for grown children who might otherwise never disclose the events in their own home lives. These are precious times and should be a part of a regular schedule so that the entire family unit and ties remain strong and united.

11. Dress up for dinner, even if you are eating in.

 When my wife and I were dating it seems like each date was an opportunity to dress up, either formally for a wedding or such, or laid back for concerts, etc. But after we married it seems like the only time we dressed up was for work and we saw each other in passing, only to quickly shed the work clothes once we came home from a long day and put on the sweats, t-shirts or pajamas. We actually forgot how much we loved the way our spouse looked all dressed up! Women need constant affirmation of how nice they look from their husbands, and we men need the same constant reminders of how delicious our wives look in a dress! So get dolled up for you mate. Dress in separate rooms and meet at a set time for diner. For a twist, add a theme and make it more fun, as in a costume party.

12. Have a snow day together, or call in and take the day off.

It is so easy to get burned out working 5-6 days per week and longing for a vacation that only comes once or twice each year. When women, and sometimes men, say "not tonight, I'm tired", it is most likely true and should not be received as a personal rejection. And yet time together in between vacations is critical to the health of a marriage. SO, why not call in sick together and stay home with a blanket without having to get ready for anything, and enjoy some quiet private time together, talking, reading, napping, or catching that chick flick she's seen 100 times before. The world won't end if you take a day off.

13. Sexting is the new thing

. Men, this will depend entirely on your wife's openness to some flirtatious fun. Most men, whether they would ever admit it, like it when they are talked dirty to, a classy woman with a trashy mouth. But we hold back from such talk with our mates for various reasons. Sending suggestive text messages is not only a fun way to use up your data allowance, but it is a relatively safe way to say things you may never feel comfortable saying in person, kind of like phone sex. Again, this does not have to lead to anything and should be appreciated and enjoyed just for the novelty of it.

But as much as it can be a turn on for us men, some women find it just as provocative and would be willing participants. In fact, it may be the only way you really find out what she likes or wants you to do with her! What a way to open up about how to please our woman for a lifetime than to give her an uncensored platform to communicate it to you in a safe and fun, non-embarrassing way.

14. Leave notes!

Everywhere! Slip a note in her favorite coffee cup; put one on her cereal box; leave a sticky on her bathroom mirror; stick one on the steering wheel of her car. Just let her know she's on your mind. And be creative! It can be as simple as "I love you, just because", or it can be playfully suggestive. Try your hand at poetry-it doesn't take much effort. For instance, "Today is payday, I made a few bucks; So this weekend I'm hoping you and I can....have intercourse". She will laugh her pants off, and if you're lucky, yours too.

15. Give her a massage.

Wow, will she ever be impressed and appreciative. If this is not in your skill set, google instructional videos on the subject and learn where the stress relieving pressure points are to totally relax and decompress her after a long week at work. Where it leads should be left totally up to her. Again, just massage her because you want to relax her and not seduce her. She will let you know how far to go-follow her lead but have no ulterior motive other than the relaxation of your honey.

16. Play off each other's sports teams.

It is not uncommon for couples to be from different parts of the country or have different allegiances to certain team. If the NFL is your sport, for instance, one might be a Cowboy fam while the other may be a Viking fan. Rivalries like this create opportunities for some fun antics and teasing, especially when one of the teams is having a much more successful year than the other. Instead of being bitter rivalries, play it up. Have a tailgate party in the living room with team logo accessories or banners. Make your partner do something like pushups whenever your team scores. Make a friendly, or naughty wager based on the outcome of the game. Don't miss this fun and often emotional opportunity to root for your favorite team at the playful and loving expense of your spouse.

These are but a few things married couples can do to make the life inside the walls of their home a little more exciting in a protected haunted house way-not knowing what's coming but feeling safe in the process. If you still have children in the home some of these suggestions can easily include them, like the indoor picnic or the kitchen food fun. But whatever you do, don't allow boredom to take up residence in your home because you are too tired or lazy to do anything to combat it. A happy wife makes for a happy life-a bored wife makes for a soon to be released sequel to the latest Unfaithful movie.

3. Chivalry Did Not Die

In Feminism

The manners and social graces true gentlemen display for others and for their wives is not a sign of weakness or subservient response, but is rooted in the code of conduct of chivalry adhered to by Knights during medieval times. The knights of the king were properly trained in all aspects of defense of country, king and the defenseless. If you were to study knighthood you would find the Ten Commandments of Chivalry. There are two of these commandments in particular from which the manners of a gentleman were derived:

Command III-Thou shalt respect all weaknesses and shalt constitute thyself the defender of them.

Command VIII-thou shalt never lie, and shalt remain faithful to thy pledged word.

While the horsemanship and warrior facets of chivalry eventually subsided, the social and moral virtues of chivalry lived on into more modern times and has become what we would refer to today and are witnessed with each act of a true gentleman.

During the 60's and 70's the feminist movement as we know it began to take shape primarily to demand and fight for equality in the work place, and the National Organization for Women was born. But as with all good movements it was hijacked by extremists whose goal was to make the roles of motherhood and housewives seem inferior to their career minded ladder climbing counterparts. Gloria Steinem became the face and the voice of the modern woman. While women have every right to feel equal to men and share similar salaries, benefits and opportunities for equal skill sets and experience, real men never felt threatened and remained chivalrous and continued on in their gentleman ways. I believe there was a misconception that simply because women wanted certain equalities they no longer wanted or needed to be treated as women. Common accts of courtesy such as holding the door for a lady became viewed by some women as an insult. As a result, some men chose to cater to this new attitude of feminism, but most men continued to display proper manners because they knew that chivalry will never go out of style.

That code of conduct or virtue set should be applied in every marriage relationship today. After all, if we want to be our mate's knight in shining armor, we need to know precisely what that code of chivalry is and when and how to display it. We need to be our wife's protector, her defender, her admirer and her faithful attender in all things marital. And she needs to know it and recognize it in you, as do your children if they are still in the home. Children mimic what they see in their fathers and are always watching us-a burden and responsibility we need to be keenly aware of. It behooves us men to learn and practice this code of proper manners with all people, but especially with our wives. But if you were not blessed to be raised in a family where you saw these or learned them from your father or from other male influences, you may not know for sure those acts of chivalry that women still appreciate, even feminists.

Whether these acts which we are about to address come natural to you or seem foreign, it will serve you well to familiarize yourself with those kindnesses that will set you apart as a true member of the royal knighthood as far as your damsel is concerned.

1. Always hold the door open for a lady.

Seems like a no-brainer but I am still amazed at how often I see a man rush into a store or restaurant right in front of a lady as if their time is more precious. And just as surprising are the looks I receive when I arrive at a door much earlier but hold the door and allow a lady to enter first. It is the only way a gentleman should act-no debate. The same would hold true for holding an elevator for someone. It's just proper and when done for your wife, it never goes unnoticed. I was guilty of not always holding the car door for my wife-I just got out of the habit-familiarity, that word again. She never minded but her response or lack of expectation should never influence my initiative to display manners. If I held the door for her when we dated I should continue to do so now.

2. Check in when away.

If you are going to be away or out for the night and you tell her you will call her to check in, then call her to check in! First it has to do with being true to your word, big in the chivalry code of conduct, and too, it lets her know you are concerned that she is safe and well while you are out. Our whereabouts should never be a secret to our spouse, and God forbid something should happen to you while you are out, an accident or injury, your wife can know where to begin her search for you based on her last conversation with you. The same holds true for women. I would never restrict her activities or suggest a curfew for her nights out, but I want to have some idea of her agenda with her understanding that it is for her safety and security should she not return home when she suggested.

3. Express Public Displays of Affection.

Public displays of affection, so common they are now referred to as PDA's, are welcomed, if tasteful. Come on men be honest with me. We know that when we are walking down the street or the mall and our wife takes our arm, we feel like a knight! Her decision to show those around that she is with her man makes us walk just a little more upright. We stick out our chest, suck in the gut and gait like a trained stallion. The same holds true for her. Let's face it, we men are visual creatures-we are easily distracted by the opposite sex, and it has nothing to do with how much or how little we love our spouse. It's an involuntary response to physical stimulus, much like Pavlov's dog-we are dogs. Our wives look too but it hurts them when we are overly fixated on other women. That is why it is so vital that other women know you are in love with the lady on your arm. Holding her hand in public, putting your arm around her waist, gentle and classy kisses go a long way in affirming your affection for her even when in a crowded room of hotties. It's also a great way to keep you focused on the one you came with so that you can be assured that she will be the one you leave with!

4. Offer your coat.

Seems like common sense but should never be ignored. If you are walking in the cool night air or in a room with the AC a bit low, take notice of your wife's discomfort and offer her your coat or jacket if she didn't bring her own. Most women chill a bit more easily than we men do and if they didn't come prepared your jacket says, "I love you". If you live in a rainy city share your umbrella with her. If it's raining and you drove, retrieve your car and pick her up at the door so she won't get soaked. Again, just simple things that should be natural protective reactions for those we love.

5. Watch where you walk when you are with her.

This is something that many men never learned or have heard of, but there is a proper way or place to walk with her depending on the situation. When walking on a street, always walk on the street side. This is for her protection should a car decide to drive on the sidewalk so that your ass gets hit but not your wife's. You may die a hero, but a chivalrous one! When going upstairs or up an escalator, she should go first with you behind her. This is not so you can have an unobstructed view of her ass-that's just an added benefit, but it is so should she fall backwards you are there to catch her. This is the old southern gentleman way. However, if you are going downstairs or down the escalator, the man should go first and be in front of the lady for much the same reason. Should she fall she would fall forward and you would be there to break her fall. It's all about her safety.

At all times the man should put himself between his wife and any potential danger.

6. Respect your wife!

Honor your wife! Admire your wife! Revere your wife! It is nearly impossible for someone to love another person they have little or no respect for. In a marriage, it's a tumor that will become untreatable if ignored. Whether you have been married to this woman for a relative short period of time or for fifty years, she deserves your respect and honor. She has devoted her life to be your lover, your helper, your supporter, your best friend and confidante. If you have children, she has given herself to raising them in ways men will never truly understand or appreciate. She may be working to help finance your dreams, or her vocation may be in keeping your house clean and in order and stomach filled. Love has many facets. Respect is one of them. In traditional wedding vows you promise to honor the other. Your vow, your promise, your good word, is among the most noble of all chivalrous characteristics.

7. Be her defender.

In tales of old the prince always comes to the rescue of the damsel in distress. In that same vow mentioned above, you promise to honor and *cherish*. Cherish simply means to lovingly protect and care for someone. That protection is displayed in a few ways. First, men, it is our duty to ensure the physical security and safety of our wives from anyone who would do her harm. We live in a twisted world where danger and harmful intent has no exclusive zip code. When we are with our mates we are the shield between them and any such danger. When we are away we leave them with that which is necessary for her to feel safe and protected. We guard our family with our lives if necessary and without hesitation.

We also defend her honor. When I was younger there was a common code among brothers. I could talk trash about my brother but anyone else who had something bad to say about him had to answer to me. Now of course in marriage you don't talk trash to your wife unless you have a nice sofa in the garage to sleep on. But under no circumstances should a man ever allow another person, male or female, to get away with disrespecting your wife, especially in public. Coming to the rescue of her honor will be received by her with the same gratitude as would coming to the rescue of her person if being threatened physically. Love, honor and cherish!

8. Exhort her always and in all things.

Compliment her on her looks all the time. If she greets you in pajamas, then tell her she rocks those PJ's. If she wakes up with bed head, then you love her natural look. If she puts on a dress or an evening gown for a night out, then tell her she looks stunning. But exhortation go beyond appearance. Maybe your wife has always wanted to play an instrument or take up singing or dancing, or write a book. If you truly take time to know your spouse, you will know their dreams. Whatever they may be, however attainable or not you may feel they are, encourage and support her in her pursuit of them and congratulate her along the way.

Take note of her contributions, her passions, her causes. Acknowledge her wisdom and seek out her advice. Make her an active partner in all important decisions-that one will come back to bite you in the ass if you fail to take heed-trust me on this.

There are so many other ways you can remain her forever knight, little things that add up and mean a lot. Let her order first when dining out. Make her coffee for her every morning. Wash her car for her. Keep the house in good repair and the landscape neatly maintained. Yes, take out the trash, yes put the seat down on the commode, yes roll the toilet paper whichever way she prefers even if it's wrong to your thinking. Your role in chivalry is to do everything within your capability to make her life safe, secure, and as carefree as possible so she can see in you the knight she craves.

4. The Lost Art of Conversation

Entire books and series of books have been written by experts on the importance of communication and conflict resolution in a marriage. Do your own research of polls and studies and you will quickly discover the three leading causes for failed marriages; sex, finances and communication. Of all the things I can look back on in my failed marriage, those things I handled poorly, my lack of effective communication and engagement with my wife is hands down number one. I'm convinced the other issues we had could have been managed if we had been able to discuss situations openly and honestly. I've written poetry, been a blogger and even spoken in front of large congregations, but I failed miserably at just talking with my spouse. I don't think I am alone in this. There is something intimidating about certain communication with our wives.

Men, we can sit around with the boys at a bar or club or backyard and talk endlessly with each other about sports, our cars, political issues or hobbies. We are never at a loss for words with our friends and time flies quickly in such settings. But when our wives ask us how our day at work went, the best we can come up with is "okay I guess". Our wives usually aren't as concerned about our work day as they are about us just showing some desire to converse with them, especially if they are young mothers who have not had an intelligent discussion beyond Sesame Street all day long.

When we were dating our wives, talk was free and easy. We were most likely attentive and eager to open up in ways that endeared them to us. We made them laugh, told jokes, shared secrets, discussed any number of topics for hours on end. But after marriage many couples face the same sudden decrease in conversation, and it tends to be our fault men. I have had many lonely hours to ponder what-ifs. If my now former wife were to ask me how things would be different if for some reason she wanted to try this again, without any hesitation the very first thing I would tell her is that I would promise to learn and apply better communication and conflict resolution skills. Of all the chapters in this short book, including the suggestive bait title, this chapter is by far the most critical and important. It matters little how much money you spend on her; how good you are in bed or how large your home is. If you can't talk to your wife, she will be tempted to find someone who will-it's that important to women! I learned this tidbit of critical information too late to save my marriage. Don't let it be so with you!

I won't presume to have all the answers to marital conversation, but I can look back and see what I did wrong and perhaps things I could have done much better, so I want to share from the perspective of someone with many regrets things I believe we men can do to enhance the lines of dialogue in our marriage. If just one of you gets it, this chapter will have served a noble purpose.

I have no desire to delve into the psyche of a woman's response or how her mind works-if I could do that accurately, I would be the first. Many with higher credentials than I have made such attempts to showcase the differences in communication styles between men and women, but I still question their accuracy. With that in mind, I prefer to keep this simple and to the point with clarity so it is easily understood and thus easily applied in your relationships.

1. Be open and willing to discuss anything-nothing should be off limits!

We chose our mates because, among other things, we felt compatible in most areas. But that should not lead to an unrealistic expectancy to agree on every single issue. Our thought processes, our wiring, our history, our upbringing are all factors in determining what we believe and how we feel about certain things. There will be times when you and your mate share opposing viewpoints on some things. It's just the way it is. For example, one of our toxic subjects was politics. I have never witnessed anything as polarizing as political ideology. It has caused riffs in families, among church members, among best friends and in marriages. I have witnessed in the recent election good people condemning other good people simply due to their preferences in how far left or right of neutral they were voting. It was embarrassing to see and feel this tension among members of my own church. But I didn't have to sleep with them! When it hit home, the attempts at discussion were so heated that I withdrew completely. I once held very strong (stubborn) party-line convictions that I believed to be vital to all humanity. How foolish I was to clam up just because my wife held different political convictions than I did. So, politics became a subject we did not ever discuss. Trust me when I tell you that avoiding hot topics is not healthy. You may believe you are avoiding controversy and therefore strengthening your marriage when in fact just the opposite is true. You have taken away one more thing that the two of you can't discuss. By the way, I now as a result give little credence to the effect of political ideologies on my life and am much more peaceful about any administration in office.

Your wife needs to feel that she can approach any subject with you on an intellectual level, even if she knows you may disagree. It is these nuances and differences that if used properly can keep things from getting stale. How boring it would be if two people agreed on every aspect of every issue without one sharpening the other with a difference of opinion. Whether the topic is politics, religion, sex, the children, careers, sports or mothers-in-law, nothing should be so potentially toxic that you should not be able to talk about it with your wife.

2. Be Open to her point of view and perspective.

This just follows the first point, but it is so easy for men to feel they are intellectually superior and that women are frail and need our unlimited knowledge and worldly experience in order for them to function. I could have learned much from my wife had I just been a bit more open to her opinions and how she came to formulate them. In most things men would probably be pragmatic where women tend to be a bit more emotional. Combining those two aspects can actually be a healthy approach as we can temper the other. We can attempt to get our spouse to consider hard data while we try to understand the emotional attachments so that together a mutual and respectful understanding can be achieved. Men, we aren't always right! Sometimes it takes a wife to point that out. Showing that you value her point of view shows her that you value her and respect her as your equal.

3. Be compassionate and attentive.

There is fewer worse feelings than trying to carry on a conversation with someone who you sense isn't paying attention to you. For all the good cell phones provide, they are also a painful distraction if your face is always buried in one, especially when with your wife. Both men and women need to be attentive and engaging in dialogue with each other. Casual banter can certainly take place over breakfast or even during a television show. But if the subject at hand is serious, then the TV needs to be turned off, the music turned down, the newspaper or video games put aside, and your phone muted so that your partner is assured that she has your complete and undivided attention. This alone goes a long way in determining the overall tone of any conversation.

By all means practice good eye contact. There is no way a man can ignore a lady if he is looking into her eyes. Her eyes in many cases will tell you what her words may leave out, so it's vital that you make eye contact with her. If the situation calls for it, hold her hand as well. The objective here is to let you know that every word or thought your wife relays is important to you and that you don't want to miss a single thing. It doesn't matter what you are discussing or how it turns out, if she can at least feel she got through to you with her feelings. Act like you care-show her it matters!

4. Let her speak without interruption.

Don't cut her off at mid-sentence or interrupt her train of thought for two reasons. First, it's just rude. Second, because women may take a long path to get to a point, we need to be attentive and allow her to lead us to that point, no matter how many detours the process takes or how many words are necessary to convey her thoughts. Men are straight shooters-we get right to the point of any discussion, just like we shop. We want socks, we go to the sock department, pick what we want and head for the cashier. Women may need hose but will stop and look at a pair of shoes that will go well with her hose, a dress that matches the color and those bathroom towels she suddenly realized she needed to trade out. The point is she will eventually get to the hose. Her conversations may indeed be very similar, which is why it is so important that a man allow his wife the time and the route that will lead to her point. I understand completely how difficult it is for men to show patience in this area, but it must be done. We cannot acknowledge the differences in communication styles between men and women without allowing them in our conversations. Patience here needs to be our friend.

5. Keep your emotions in check and your defenses down when the dialogue heats up.

This was another area where I failed miserably. Mind you women need to understand how to and how not to open any conversation with a man, but how easy it is for us to go on the defensive when presented with a strong offense. It's not football, it conversation. When we respond emotionally or get defensive due to the tone, the pitch or the subject matter of a discussion, we fail to apply any of the Do's we just

47

covered. We fail to listen, we cut her off midstream, we dismiss her point of view, and we certainly lay the groundwork for another topic that is off the table. Men can be very logical in their thinking until someone challenges them in any way. We see this on social media all the time. We are all arm chair experts behind a computer screen. But whenever someone challenges our opinion, all the rationale that we are known for is tossed out the window and we are ready for a battle of words like a well-trained debate team member. Our wives will have emotion enough for the both of you without you disregarding all reasoning because your emotions just hijacked the conversation. With everything that is within us we need to maintain a meekness, that is a controlled strength, and be vulnerable with our wives even when we may feel under attack. We are not in a bar room brawl, but a disagreement with the person we share life with. It's great that men can be emotional in front of their women, but not when the emotions are negative and directed toward our loving spouses. Don't allow a heated exchange to become a potential crime of passion over a simple disagreement.

6. Don't assume she is asking you to fix something!

Men like to tinker with things. We fix stuff-it's what we do. Our natural response to a given or expressed concern is to quickly determine how to remedy the situation. This however, doesn't always work with conversations with our wives. We by nature assume that if she is wanting to share something with us that troubles her, then she wants us to advise her as to how to fix it. But more times than not, she just needs to vent and bend your ear. If we automatically go into Mr. Fix-it mode, we completely lose sight of what she is sharing and miss out on a tremendous opportunity to just be a compassionate support for her. Don't grab for your tool belt whenever she starts a serious conversation with you. Just listen!

7. Timing is everything!

Men want their mates to understand the hallowed ground of the family room on a Sunday afternoon when our football games are on, or for that matter, most anytime any of our teams are on TV. Smart women know from experience when it is unproductive and unreceptive to attempt dialogue with us. Men need to learn this same art of proper timing when we are the ones needing to talk. Just as we don't think clearly when our team has the ball first and goal, women aren't ready to make intelligent conversation during Sex in the City or their 50th viewing of You've Got Mail. It's not even wise to suggest to her during a commercial break that you need to chat with her because she will then be distracted for the balance of her show and be resentful that you planted the seed just before her TV lovers are about to meet. There are few things that men need to discuss with their spouses that can't wait until you have her attention. Learning this lost art will encourage her to do the same with you.

In summary learning how to have positive interaction with your wife will save you a world of heartache and give both of you a platform of comfort in knowing you can share your innermost thought, fears or concerns with the other and be shown love, support and respect, regardless the topic. Love can be the ultimate communication when words are not needed, but there will be many times when words and dialogue need to be employed. We men need to know the difference and be prepared and willing to engage in open and honest communication when times call for it. Later in another chapter we will address conflict resolution or learning when and how to fight fair. But properly applied, these preceding steps in knowing how to talk now will save most men from having to fight later.

5. Those "Just Because" Tokens

Most women love the slightest display of thoughtfulness. Any mom will take that pulled-up dandelion weed from her three-year old son's dirty hands and receive it as if it were a dozen long-stemmed roses from the most expensive florist in town. Ask her to pull out his scrapbook when he's grown, and that little yellow weed will most likely be pressed between the pages because it meant something special to her. It wasn't the weed-it was the thought behind the gesture! When I was married my wife saved virtually every bouquet of roses I ever bought her and dried them upside down in her walk-in just to keep them. They had no value as dead wilted dried-up flowers, but they represented a thoughtful "just because" moment or occasion that she chose to save and view every day.

When men are in love and it's still fresh, it's almost natural even for us to bring home little gifts or pick up a rose when we're at the grocery store and bring home like that little boy and his dandelion weed, just because we were thinking about our new love. I would rarely travel out of town without bringing back some small memento from the city I was visiting just so she would know I was thinking about her while I was away. Once I learned about things she liked to collect it was easy to see something, assume she would like it, and buy it just because. For example, she liked to collect miniature ceramic shoes, so I would always find one or two for her while I was away.

But as with many other rituals and customs in a long-term marriage, this ended or at least subsided to some degree. In any other aspect of our life, our career, our hobbies, playing an instrument, watching our diet, when something obviously works, we continue doing it to achieve the desired results. But in marriage the things we did to win our bride and capture her heart, the things that obviously worked, are all too soon discontinued. It usually isn't a case of not caring-we love our wives-it's more a case of comfort, familiarity settling in and getting lazy in our efforts to keep things alive and fresh. We may feel like we don't have to work so hard at showing our love because by this time she should have a clue, right?

It is so crazy how much of an impact it has on your spouse to show some small token of thoughtfulness and how easy it should be for us men to do. I liken it to church attendance; those who go for Christmas and Easter may not be spiritually healthy the other 363 days of the year compared to those who go regularly. Likewise, if you only show signs of sentiment on Valentine's Day, your Wedding Anniversary and her birthday, you are missing out on opportunities for you to show, and for her to see, that you care and think of her every day of the year and that you want to keep your marriage healthy.

I can almost hear some men now saying, "my wife knows I love her". You would be missing the point. You know your kids and maybe if like me, your grandkids love you. But when they crawl up into your lap and wrap their little arms around your neck and tell you that they love you, it melts even the hardest of hearts. When my grandkids would visit me in my office it would make even the most difficult of days suddenly beautiful! Knowing it is great-feeling it is priceless!

Words are definitely important, as discussed earlier in honing our communication skills. Our wives should always hear words of endearment coming from us. But these little "just because" tokens represent a thought that spurred an action with the purpose of representing some little tangible display that backs up our words. It truly can be the little things that count, especially when done without our wife hinting or outright asking. Men should know this when they witness the response to a gift that costs us little but sparks an unexpected response of gratitude as if we'd just spent a paycheck on them. If you don't practice this and your wife doesn't seem to care, you are being fooled. She notices when you do little things and she notices when you fail to. If you aren't really sure, it's safest to just hedge your bet and comply. Call it love insurance-it may not seem important but comes in handy during a marital catastrophe.

As for practical application, it's quite simple. First, if married, you should know her pretty well by now. If not, you aren't paying attention or doing your due diligence. All men should know their wives favorite color, favorite perfume, her preferred candy bar, her music preference, if she's into things like miniature animals, certain books, favorite authors, favorite flower, Sports allegiance, etc. When you pay attention to the details *of* her life you reaffirm her importance *in* your life. Simple example-you are at the grocery store in the checkout lane and see her favorite candy bar, a Milky Way. It's a no-brainer-you grab one and take it home to her. She's impressed, mission accomplished. But same scenario, you grab a Butterfinger for her-trust me-she will show grace but will wonder why you didn't know to get Milky Way instead. It's these subtle nuances that separate the very successful relationships from the ones that are common and uninspiring.

What are some other examples of these "just because" tokens besides candy? Of course, all women love flowers-a single rose can go a long way and in some cases, is actually more romantic than a full bouquet. Coming home with flowers for no special reason other than her, never gets old! Maybe her favorite group just released a new project-buy her the CD before she does. Want to make a lasting impression and score huge brownie points, surprise her with tickets when her band is playing in your town. Maybe she's a sports fanatic like you and has a favorite team. Any little item from her team that you bring home will be stored away in a special place. It can even be used in a playful way when each have rival teams.

Sometime tokens can be more practical. Stop on the way home and grab take-out so she doesn't have to cook. Just be sure to let her in on your intentions. This could go bad if you try to surprise her only to find she's halfway through her meal preparation. Take-out doesn't need to be expensive. Pizza and cheap wine can make for a well-received gesture. Food may not seem like a token-it isn't. It's the not having to cook for you that is the token.

And I believe every husband should have a pad or two of sticky notes just for leaving them around for wives. If you don't have any, spend a buck and get different colors. You can even order them online preprinted with hearts, flowers, pets, etc. Leave a note beside her coffee cup in the morning. Place one on the steering wheel of her car. Sneak one into her purse if you dare. Play games with them and leave a trail of clues as to where you are or where you want her to be. These are so mindless but effective in communicating loving words and thoughts with your wife. She'll be giddy like a little girl when you use these effectively.

As for what to write on them, be creative and mix it up. They can be simple and meaningful things like "I love you", "I'll be thinking about you today", "I hope you have a great day hon", etc. Others can be light or even suggestive, like "Any after dinner plans?", or "I still love watching you walk out of a room slowly", or "where would you like breakfast?". The more daring of men can take it to the level of poetry or limericks. Whatever your approach, handwritten notes "just because" done sincerely are highly effective in keeping on your wife's good side.

Along the same line of thought, create for her some Love coupons. These are popular during Valentine's Day but can be easily duplicated with notes. Ideas for these coupons might be something like One free hug redeemable any time, or a foot massage at her request, one night of music and dancing in the living room, an extra 30 minutes of alone time before bed, or, one of the more popular, Free Babysitting so she can have a night out with the girls. (Fathers should never really refer to watching their own children as babysitting, by the way). Encouraging her to get out of the house without you and the kids can be very healthy for your relationship. More on that later. In any event, these Love Coupons are fun and highly appreciative.

Seems everyone these days lives by their cell phones. Like the old American Express commercial, we never leave home without it. What a better instrument to use for tokens of love. Surprise your wife on occasion with a simple text. Like sticky notes they can be sentimental, they can be funny or flirtatious. When your wife receives a text from you in the middle of her day, you can't imagine the warmth and fuzzy feelings it creates just knowing you at that moment are thinking about her. Use your phone to make her smile.

There are so many "Just Because" opportunities in any relationship if you are paying attention. Looking for and taking advantage of these moments should be done so often that it becomes your second nature. Buy her a card in between occasions for no reason. Write something in it from your heart in your own words-short but sincere. Wish her a Happy Tuesday! Wash her car for her on the weekend while she's doing something else. Fill it up with a tank of gas for her. Draw her a bubble bath, put on some music, light a couple candles and then leave her alone for some quiet time while you clean the kitchen. Paint her toe nails for her. She will really love you for this one-just do a good job! They will be seen in public! Brush her hair out for her some night before bed.

I hope you are getting the point. You don't have to be wealthy or go out of your way to do or buy something every day; this might actually be counter-productive and could even take away from the novelty of the gesture. But just find opportunities to let her know by subtle reminders and "just because" displays of thoughtfulness that she is still on your mind, and not just because you like her butt. And by all means, please do these things without expected reciprocation. We don't give to get, we don't spoil to be spoiled and we don't love just to be loved in return. Those responses will occur naturally when you are sincere in your affection. Words mean much but words affirmed by deeds make for a better conviction. I remember an old tune back in the day about a failed romance, with a line, You Don't Sing Me Love Songs, You Don't Bring Me Flowers Anymore. Don't be that guy!

6. Just Looking for Some Touch

If you are a classic rock fan you may recall an old ZZ Top song entitled Just Looking for some Tush, although most thought the word was 'touch". But the truth is all of us love and need human touch. It is wired into our nature from the very first day of birth when we're laid on our mother's breast. It has been studied and proven that premature infants who are held regularly gain weight much quicker than those left alone in a crib. Human touch is healthy.

Men we see this all the time without thinking about it. Watch your favorite sports team make a big play and they will hug each other or give a high-five. Make the big play and the coach will slap your ass when you're walking off the court or grab the back of your neck in an approving manner. I'm a hugger-I hug my male friends in the bar, at church, when I run into them on the street. My grown sons all get hugs from their dad unashamedly. We have no problem touching each other-it's a natural response. Love begets affection!

In the same way, our wives love touch. Touch communicates when words are few and unnecessary. She can probably tell you where you both were when you first held her hand or put your arm around her. She will definitely and fondly remember that very first kiss. Affection is so vitally important in any relationship and is the life blood of kindled hearts. It allows two hearts to occupy one single space in that the two in every way become one. For many men this comes naturally while for others, it may seem awkward. I would guess it has much to do with the affection shown in your home when you were growing up, both in the affection you received and with displays of affection you witnessed between your parents...or not. One of the best things a man can do for his children is to allow them to see and witness your affection for their mother! They will learn to mimic it later in their own relationships.

I'm giving away my age when I say how much fun dating was back when the older cars still had bench seats and your date could sit next to you before bench seats were replaced with bucket seats. You could have your date sit next to you, hold her hand or place yours on her leg while driving. I'm convinced the divorce rate increased when bench seats in cars went away. Maybe I should do a study someday. It's amazing how many of us survived driving with only lap belts three across on a bench seat compared to the modern three-point restraint. Safety concerns had much to do with the decrease of touch in everyday tasks like taking a drive in the country or parking in your favorite lovers' lane. I have fond memories of dates in an old 1972 Pontiac Catalina with a big-ass front seat, most of which will remain locked away forever in the recess of my memory, things of the past like that old bench seat. Those days are gone.

I don't need to explain the physical thrill of sexual touch. We will delve into that a bit later in another chapter. What I'm referring to in this chapter is everyday non-sexually motivated touch, brushes, nibbles, strokes and caresses. When two people are in love for the first time they can hardly keep their hands off the other. Whether holding hands, walking arm-in-arm or just sitting close, they are always in touch with each other and almost sense pain when they are separated for any period of time. Physical affectionate touch is an addictive drug with many positive benefits as related to a healthy relationship. And when withheld it can be the driving force behind infidelity-it's that important. There is comfort in the touch of your mate. There is a sense of security when lying in bed and being able to reach and touch the other person and feel at peace knowing they are close by. Again, there is non-verbal communication that takes place when touch is exchanged. There are highly charged sensations at the soft strokes of deliberate fingers. Touch is very important in any relationship between two people.

Intimacy between couples does not always equate to sex. I'm hoping by now you are picking up on that and how the title of the book supports this notion. And yet it is the everyday touches that keeps your wife's senses on alert and it can lead to a more fulfilling sexual experience. Conversely if a man displays little or no affection for his wife throughout the day and week he should not expect much of a stimulating sex life because he hasn't kept the embers glowing that spark the flame of passion later. It's a bit like jumping into a car that hasn't been running on a very cold night but expecting it to be instantly warm when you turn the key. It never works like that.

In addition to domestic affection, public displays of affection, or more commonly referred to now as PDA's, are also important to our wives. She may know through your home life that you love her, but nothing gives her more of a sense of pride and security in a relationship than for her man to openly and lovingly kiss her or hold her close when in public situations as if she is the only person in the room and in your world. In her mind you are letting everyone around you know that you are indeed in love with this woman, and that you are humbled to be hers and not ashamed to show it. And in an animalistic sort of way, you are letting others know that she's your mate and spoken for and that you, her alpha male will take down anyone who would challenge that notion. Of course, these PDA's need to be in good taste and respectful to your wife- no ass grabbing or tonsil fishing unless there is a room to rent close by. Overt or over the top displays will make her uncomfortable and put her in a potentially embarrassing situation, especially around her friends. People, especially women, can spot a phony. So, sincerity is your best friend in your affectionate overtures.

As eluded to earlier, depending on how you were raised or what you were exposed to, affection may not come naturally to some men. Some have been taught that if you are loving and affectionate outside of sex then you must relinquish your Man Card. Please, for the sake of your marriage, don't buy into that. But if showing affection doesn't come natural to you, don't worry-there's good news for you-it's not that complicated. But if you're still uncomfortable, try these simple but effective methods of loving touch.

Assuming you sleep in the same bed (some couples don't) give her a thirty-second morning hug before you or she gets up to get ready for work. But keep it simple and remember, your morning breath probably smells as bad as hers does. A loving embrace before jumping in the shower is a great way to start any day. Set the alarm for five minutes earlier and use the snooze button as an opportunity to wake up together.

Along the title of the book, if she's in the kitchen preparing meals, slip up behind her and gently kiss the back or nape of her neck-no hickeys. Or put your arm around her and give her a hug from behind. Displays of affection in areas designated for other uses, like cooking, just let her know that wherever she is or whatever she's doing, you love her. It just might get you an extra piece of bacon or a little more butter in your taters.

When out shopping or painting the town take her hand in yours. Don't lead her, just hold her. You can also take her hand and place it in your arm as you walk or put your arm around her waist or shoulders. Again, this is simply another form of public affirmation of your feelings for her. It also plays into the afore mentioned chivalry. Little things.

At the end of a long day if you watch television together place her feet on your lap and give her a gentle foot massage. This will score all kinds of husband points for you! Not only will she appreciate the sentiment but there are so may pressure response points in the foot that directly affect other parts of the body that she will be totally relaxed and the proverbial putty in your hands. Along the same thought, have her sit on the floor in front of you and give her a gentle shoulder massage.

Stroke her hair! Go slow and easy-you will ruin the moment if you get your fat fingers tangled in it or if heaven forbid, you mess it up. If she has longer hair offer to brush it out for her before she goes to bed. If you are really bold learn how to braid her hair. Not only will you be giving her attention, you will be doing something for her that she would have to do for herself if you weren't there. Again, it's just such a simple but to her, a meaningful gesture.

Back to the sofa, let her put her head on your lap while watching a movie. If she falls asleep don't take it personally-it is actually the ultimate compliment of her feeling of safety and security with you. A woman who can fall asleep on her man is a happy and contented woman. Don't be offended-eat it up.

Offer to give her a massage or rub down-no strings attached as we discussed earlier. It can be a vigorous pressurized session if you've studied and know what you're doing, or it can simply be a soft caressing of her neck, back and shoulders. Her moans will tell you where she hurts as well as where she feels good! Once you learn your way around nerves and muscles you will be able to sense areas where she is tight and do your magic. Everyone feels stress and most stress is centered around the spine or in the shoulders. There are few things more satisfying than a good massage by someone who knows what they are doing. To be able to do this for your wife will not only achieve the objective of loving touch but will relax her in ways you may never know, and she will be impressed and appreciative of your attention and efforts.

And just one more thing-hug your wife-often. It does as much for the man as it does the wife. There is again, a non-verbal exchange of communication that happens when two people in love just hold each other. It's an act that doesn't require words. It comforts when one is sad, it affirms when one needs to know your love, it heals and sooths after a long and stressful day and it brings to focus the heart, the core of emotions and feelings that are the indicators of the unspoken souls. Hug your woman, when you awake, when you get home from work, before you retire for the night.

The importance of displaying affection in a loving relationship cannot be over emphasized, whether it's hugging your children, kissing your elderly father or holding your wife. Everybody wants to be touched. It is through human touch that love can be transferred without words.

7. Work That Vacuum Boy-ee!

I saw a meme once that read "there is nothing sexier than a man with a vacuum cleaner". I might add to that there is no bigger turn-off that a dirty or cluttered home. But for some reason many men think that house chores are the responsibility of the women and with the exception of taking out the trash when asked for the third time or cutting the grass once per week, house cleaning isn't their job. There's a joke that goes something like, a man knows what you want him to do around the house-you don't need to remind him every six months! A house may be the man's castle but if you want to keep the Princess singing like a Disney movie you need to help with the everyday tasks of domesticity. We don't fully appreciate how overwhelming it is for a lady who works outside of the home all day to come home to a house that is cluttered by kids at play while you are sitting in your recliner asleep or watching a game oblivious to your surroundings. The sad thing is that many of us men have lived alone at some point in our life, either in college or later as a bachelor, and we had no one to do our laundry, clean the kitchen or cook our meals, except us! So, we know we are capable of domestic engineering. And yet when we get married we somehow get this epiphany that the woman we love and married has now become our maid service.

Now that I've been living alone in the house I once shared with my wife, it's amazing to me how much more I notice when everything is covered in dust, certain smells I never noticed before (presumably because someone cleaned them before they began to omit aromas), and why sheets need to be washed more than once every other month. Some men may be phobic when it comes to cleanliness, but most of us could live life in an Animal House type dorm and be okay with it.   But keeping a clean house isn't just about cleanliness, women are turned off by a filthy home. A man should use this knowledge to his advantage and make house cleaning fun and maybe even playful.

What honest man can deny having thoughts or fantasies about their lady cleaning house in a tiny French maid outfit. We've all seen the pictures and don't pretend you haven't. So, who can say that a woman may not get similar vibes when she comes home to her man not only putting on a show but doing something that the wife will not have to do herself! A home is not only the man's castle. The wife too considers it her refuge, the place where she can unwind after work without the burden of picking up dirty clothes, emptying the dishwasher or cleaning up spills before she can kick back. The upkeep of the home should be a shared responsibility if a man truly wants a happy wife. Neglect in this area will cause eventual resentment in a wife that may not show right away but will fester like a sore that won't heal. Nothing good can come from living with a pig of a husband whose house would look like his dorm room if he had his way.

Much of a woman's identity is attached to her home. If you are a couple who entertains much you will witness the hours she can put into cleaning floors, polishing flatware, dusting of all the surfaces in every room, pictures, frames, etc.

I know that before any family gatherings such as holidays I might as well not plan anything for the day before because we were going to be in cleaning mode. If the floors of a lady's house are dirty she takes it as a personal reflection on her grade as a wife and caretaker. Even with two dogs there was no way anyone would ever walk into our home for a dinner or get together and see any dirt on the floors, baseboards, or any other surface. The same zealous attitude men show for their mancave is the same women show for their dollhouse. On the other hand, if a man could consider how much care he takes in keeping his classic Hot Rod clean and polished, he will have a clearer understanding of how a woman considers the cleanliness of her home.

Cleanliness is healthy and most certainly a virtue. I will admit that I detested these cleaning sprees because I knew going in how intense they would be. But I also have to admit that when it was all said and done, there really was a feeling of accomplishment knowing that the entire house was thoroughly cleaned and that the lady of the house was satisfied with the results. I learned quickly that not only would my wife be pleased that I assisted in helping around the house, but she would as a result have more energy reserved for me later-it was a win-win. The sooner married men understand this, the better the marriage will be. Take care of her house and she will be more inclined to take care of you.

And in keeping with the title of the book, there are other benefits to a home with clean surfaces. You are watching a movie together in the family room when the spontaneous urge hits and you decide the carpeted floor will do. But she quickly switches channels due to the hair and debris on a carpet that hasn't been vacuumed in two weeks and one of your dirty socks under the sofa so long she mistakes it for a rodent.

Or you may be in the kitchen and decide to plant your lady on the counter for a quick snack, but she suddenly loses her appetite because of the food crumbs she's sitting on or the cold liquid invading her crack from a spill that didn't get wiped up. Mud wrestling may be acceptable in cowboy bars but fun in the dirt will not fly in the home of a married couple. No amount of emergency cleaning will recover the spark of spontaneity once the moment is gone due to unsanitary surfaces.

Women see things men don't or won't pay attention to. They will find dust on picture frames, the dirt on base boards, the dust lines in drapes, and even or especially hair in the bed sheets. It seems to be a trait shared by most women I know and two I've been married to. If there is a crack or crevice that can attract dust a woman will sniff it out like a blood hound until it is removed. Smart men will make note of this and pay attention when shopping for accessories like wall sculptures or elaborate frames that require liquid air for proper cleaning. It seems the more curves and detail a piece has the more your wife will want it in her home. When you clean, don't take shortcuts-you won't be fooling her and it will only come back on your lack of detail.

The objective here is to do your part or more in keeping the house clean and reducing the domestic cleaning responsibility on your wife. This isn't to say that if you work long hours you need to spend every night cleaning. But neither should your wife! Some things can wait until the weekend. If your wife has a day when she does the laundry, then use that time to help with house chores. Other things, spills, stains on the rugs, etc. need immediate attention. If cleaning is not your gift it will serve you well to invest in a book on How to Clean Anything. There are several editions in print and you can research any cleaning related concern online as well. Have an arsenal of supplies on hand for those times when a stain calls for soda or citrus cleaner. Don't improvise if you have no clue what you are doing. Learn the cleaning factor of certain fabrics so when you shop together for floor coverings or furniture you are buying something that doesn't require professional dry cleaning. Do your homework, and make your house an easy-maintenance environment that even you can handle.

In my opinion, there are some things a man should never ask a woman to do when it comes to domestic cleanliness. We have always had dogs and dogs always leave little tokens of their appreciation in the yard. That was always my job, period. There was just something gross to me about having my lovely wife picking up dog droppings. A man should always take out the trash and put it out for pickup on the appropriate days. A man should always rinse out the tub or spray down the shower to get rid of body hair that collects on the shower walls or around the drain. Women don't want to play with nasty soap entangled hair vermin we leave behind. And men, please do your mate the courtesy of keeping the toilets cleaned, especially the one you both share. There are just certain things a wife should never be expected to get used to!

When a man lives alone, with no one else in the residence to take care of him, he takes care of himself. Perhaps some men more efficiently than others, but somehow, we manage. If we don't want the trash to overflow, we empty it; if we don't want mold growing on our dirty dishes, we clean them or put them in the dishwasher. When we run out of clean underwear we do a load of laundry. We do what we must to maintain some sense of neatness and cleanliness. If we take the same approach after we marry, that is we continue to do what we've always done for ourselves, then marital domestication should never pose a challenge for us or create an issue with our wives-pretty simple.

If you love your mate, if you want her to love you back, if you desire her to have desires for you at the end of the day or week, step up to the plate and help her keep a clean, healthy and adventure friendly domicile. Just remember nothing says sexy more to a woman than a man cleaning her house! If you want to put that theory to the test, tell your lover that you will meet her in the bedroom, after you fold and put away the clothes!

8. Flattery Will Get You Everywhere

We discussed in an earlier chapter the importance of communication. Even the men who are better communicators don't talk nearly as much during the course of a normal day as women do. I believe I read somewhere that women speak on average around seven thousand words daily compared to two thousand for men. If this is close to accurate it is important that men are deliberate in complimenting their mates with all sincerity. Some studies indicate that men who shower their wives with many more positive comments than negative ones tend to have much longer and more successful marriages.

Men are typically creatures who are stimulated visually, which would explain the continuing popularity of non-contact gentlemen clubs. We can be "moved" at the mere sight of a nice ass with no words, no sound and no contact. Sir Mix-a-Lot had it right. While women certainly appreciate the same visual stimuli, their real juices get flowing when their emotions are stirred by affirming comments given by their men. For many women, intimacy begins with words and compliments. You would think men would find it easier to flatter their wives than it really appears to be. Again, men are not the most expressive in matters of the heart or intimacy. Ask men to describe a square box and we will say it has four equal square sides, a top and a bottom. Ask a woman and she will also describe the corners, the shadows of each side depending on the light source, the color of the box, how the box feels, how much it weighs, what kind of tape is being used to hold the box together and if it has any odors coming from inside. She will describe the types of items that would fit into the box and how many would fit in her closet. We communicate differently for sure. Once men can truly grasp the importance of words to a woman he will have much more success in his relationship.

Compliments can come in a variety of ways and address a multitude of positive traits in your mate. I'd like to offer some examples of compliments women want and need to hear, along with the reason these particular comments mean so much to them. You can use your own words, but you will get the point.

"Our kids are so lucky to have you for their mom."

Men will never fully appreciate the bond between a mother and her children. A mom almost always wonders if she's doing enough, if she's doing it right, if her kids or her husband ever take notice of the work and sacrifice she puts into being a mom, the love she packs into nightly meals or lunches, the concerns she has for their welfare, etc. Your children are the blessing of your physical and emotional union. It is not only important that she hears and knows that she is a good mom, it's important to her that you see it and find it valuable and attractive and yet another reason for you to love her. It's also important that your children hear you compliment her mothering, so they too are more aware of her loving sacrifices for the family.

"You are such a good cook".

Hopefully this is true enough. I have seen that even with career minded women, there is still a desire to be skillful at "womanly" things. The old cliché that the best way to a man's heart is through his stomach still holds true for many women. I believe they not only want to know that they have mad cooking skills, but that their planned nightly menus and the preparation of your meals is received as nourishment for the heart and body and that you love every morsel. This is especially true if her skills are still being honed. Burnt macaroni actually tastes pretty good!

"I love looking into your eyes".

This was an easy one for me as my wife had beautiful blue eyes that looked like polished glass marbles-it was the second thing that attracted me to her. Through the years as our bodies aged, her eyes retained that same sparkle. At the heart of good conversation is direct eye contact. She needs to hear that you love looking at her eyes whether you are newlyweds or if you have aged well together. Her eyes are a true gauge of what's going on deep inside. They can tell you things she doesn't verbalize. Let her hear that her eyes still mystify you.

"I was thinking about you today".

This is pretty self-explanatory. What woman young or old doesn't delight in the thought that she is still on her man's mind. Knowing that when you are apart you still think of her is an affirmation statement that she will never get tired of hearing. It may also create a sense of curiosity-what were you thinking? Of her love-her smile, her curves, the previous night of passion? Let her wonder, but make it known by your comments that in some form or fashion, she was on your mind while you worked or played.

"Wow, you are breath-taking in that dress".

Getting dressed for any occasion is generally a snap for a man. White or blue shirt, black or grey suit, matching shoes, one of five ties we own-a piece of cake. Or in some cases, your wife will tell you what to wear and make it even easier. But, I can't begin to describe the process of elimination women go through in finding the right dress, matching it with the shoes, liking the shoes better than the dress so changing the dress only to find the matching purse she thought she had for the shoes is missing, which starts the whole process over again. By the time she finally feels presentable, the very first words out of any man's mouth who has the least bit of compassion and self-preservation, better be complimentary.

But beyond that we mentioned earlier how infrequent it sometimes becomes for couples to dress up to go out compared to when they were dating. It is easy for us men to forget how lovely our wives are in an attractive well-cut dress. If she goes through the process just described without aa single glance or acknowledgment from you on her apparel choice, it will be a long night and you will most likely have no clue why. Remember this-*if she's in a dress you must express!*

"I would do it all over again".

It's common these days for couple to renew their wedding vows once they reach a certain milestone, like a tenth or twenty-fifth anniversary. It is your way of letting your friends and family, and your spouse know that you made the right choice and you are still committed to the marriage. But a smart man will not wait every ten years or so to let her know this little tidbit. Having her close and letting her know forthright just how lucky you are to be with such an incredible woman is simply another one of those affirming moments she will never grow weary of. It's vital that men show their partners everyday how blessed they are to be together, but it must be followed up with confirming words because again, a woman is moved to intimacy through love language. Words mean so much more to her when they are in concert with your actions.

"I can't wait to get you alone".

A couple should never be together so long or so boringly familiar with each other that suggestive or provocative comments are deemed obsolete. Any woman of any size, ethnicity, any degree of education, any amount of corporate success. Still needs to hear from her man that she is desirable to him.

Say what you will about all the qualities you found attractive about her when you first fell in love, there is always a physical attraction. Whether you are a butt man, a breast man, into long blonde hair or longer legs, there was something in her physical appearance that first grabbed your attention. It is easy through the years for a woman to question her appeal, particularly after bearing children and having a difficult time finding that high school figure she once had. It's even more difficult when her man refuses to offer her any affirmation of his purely sexual desire for her. You need to be deliberate with your positive comments regarding the way she still turns you on, the anticipation you still feel at the thought of making love to her, and the desire or even cravings you still have for her body. Don't wait until you are in bed to seduce her with words-be seducing her all day, all week. Seductive comments don't have to imply immediate gratification, but when you do come together (okay, maybe pun intended), intimacy will be much more gratifying for you both.

"I love your little freckles".

It might be freckles, it might be dimples, maybe a mole or it may be a scar or birthmark, but many women have areas of their body that they view as imperfections. In extreme cases maybe your wife has an amputation or has scars from a mastectomy to save her life. Whether your wife had these "imperfections" before you married her or has battle wounds that occurred much later, men should not ignore these areas of her body but rather embrace them. For women, a man completely ignoring the obvious implies to her that you find whatever it is to be unattractive, therefore you never mention it. This may not be true, but women will have this perception. However, if you acknowledge and embrace and even celebrate an old scar from a bad burn, or freckles that would make a cute picture if connected. You are telling your wife that nothing in your wife's appearance is detestable or a turn-off for you and that in fact, it only serves to make her even more unique. Don't shy away from lovingly paying attention to areas of her body she may pretend she would rather you didn't. Truth be told men, we all have the same areas.

"As usual hon, you were right".

Wives certainly want to feel physically desirable but it's also important that they are valued for their intelligence. I heard a single lady on a radio talk show recently state that if she's been on a date with some guy, the first few compliments about her appearance are appreciated and well received. But after a couple hours in, if he is still simply commenting on her looks, but isn't engaging her in any conversation of substance, she will begin to be turned away. A woman's physical appeal is just one facet of affirmation she seeks from her man. She needs to feel her opinions matter, she wants to know her input is considered in family decisions, and she needs to be convinced that you love her for her mind just as much as you do for any other part of her. This would be even more true in matters where perhaps the two of you disagreed on an important topic and her preference or opinion ended up being the correct one. Love her for her mind and tell her so. Remember, the brain is her largest sex organ!

"I really appreciate the way you..."

Truth be told most wives are saints for the way they take care of us men and put up with our hang-ups. Even career women find the time to do the family laundry, ironing, wash dirty sheets, make the beds, and other wifely chores that she may not want to relinquish to a man, just because. If there is cooking or baking required for Thanksgiving or other holidays, she will be the one most likely to bring the goods. If the children are sick, she will be the one mothering them back to health. There are so many things a wife does for her family that may not be directly related to the marriage relationship but has positive impact on every facet of it. We need to be sure to take every opportunity to let them know we see them, we notice, we appreciate and value every act and that it only serves to increase our love for them. When someone gives all they can to enhance the lives of others but receives no acknowledgment or mention from time to time, it will wear on you-I know. It's not her duty to take care of you, it's her choice! Acknowledging this often will never grow old to her-she will always appreciate hearing from you that you take notice of the little things. "Honey I love the fact that I always have clean shirts for work" or "babe, your meals are better than any restaurant". Be appreciative of the things she may not think you notice.

"Your Kiss is on my list…".

Yes, it made for a great hit record back in the day. I am a firm believer-extremely convicted that when a couple no longer desires to kiss each other, not the have-a-good-day variety, but the passionate second date kind, the marriage will fade into monotony if it survives at all! Say what you want about great sex, simultaneous orgasms, frequency that would make newlyweds jealous-it is a passionate kiss that acts as the window to the soul, and in my opinion the most intimate exchange between two people who love each other. If the makers of the little blue pill knew the power of a deep passionate kiss, they would sell off their stock for fear that others would eventually figure out the positive impact on the male libido that a wet and warm kiss can make-for free! Ask any couple and they will always tell you when they first kissed, and how it was, and for the female, how long she thought about it that night. A kiss can be non-sexual and still afford the greatest degree of fulfillment, or it can be the catalyst that turns a physical response into a near spiritual euphoric encounter that two people feel was created just for them and no one else. Have I adequately explained my view on the importance of kissing your wife? It is the one thing I sincerely miss more than sex. It was the one thing that confirmed the feelings I suspected I had for her. It is the one thing I remember most of all our physical encounters. I will be forever grateful for her kiss and forever tormented without it. Men, kiss your wives and do it like a boss with passion. I need to end this chapter here and go take a cold shower.

9. Allow Her to Fly

While writing this book I came across a survey on a popular social media site asking the question, are men intimidated by career minded or successful women. Our parents may never have asked such questions because during the 50's and 60's successful women working outside of the home was not an issue to be considered. Granted many women took jobs in factories during World Wars I and II, by the 50's most women had settled back into their roles of taking care of the home and kids while the man resumed the duty of bread winner. This is 2017-times have changed.

Women have fought long and hard to have an equal share in the success of a chosen career or vocational path. Glass ceilings have crumbled, wages are more equitable and good ol' boys clubs are vanishing. Some may argue that there is still much work to do but in the course of historical comparison, women have come a long way, baby!

Not all ladies desire careers outside of the home. Many find fulfillment and joy in the full-time vocation of a domestic wife or the noble calling to be a stay-at-home mom. Those women should never be made to feel like under achievers or those not living up to their full potential, in fact just the opposite is true. The world is a better place because of women fully devoted to their respective families, and for most every successful man in his chosen profession, there is a loving and supportive and encouraging woman waiting for him at the end of a long day.

With that said, many are the women who do have dreams or aspirations of being successful or finding fulfillment in some vocation or art or gifting outside the confines of domestication. All of us have dreams. Some of us have regrets for not following those dreams. From early on in life we find those things that interest us or pull at us to explore and develop. Those dreams may be as high as being professional athletes or competing in the Olympics or becoming a recording star. For others it may be to earn a degree in a chosen field of study like law or medicine. Still others may hope to be the best local interior designer or a published author. The point is if we live, we dream, and if we are cognizant, those dreams never really die.

All men in relationships should know their mates well enough to know her deepest desires or dreams. If you don't, you simply aren't paying enough attention to her. It is those dreams that drive her. I know it may be difficult to accept, but men, all women don't live solely for their husbands! They need to be allowed to blossom, to sprout wings and fly!

Men should never feel intimidated by a woman with a passion to succeed. It should be just the opposite. Some studies suggest that many become successful by migrating to other successful people. If you are fortunate enough to be married to someone with a drive and a goal, their habits may be a good thing for you in your endeavors as well. There should exist a mutual commitment to exhort each other on to the desired results and goals in order to have a terrific marriage with no limits. One of the most loving and sexiest things a man can ask his wife is simply, "hon, what do you really want to do? What is your dream?' "What, if anything, can I do to help make that dream come true?"

When men become intimidated at the thought of his woman having goals or dreams, it may be due to one of a few things. It might simply be a matter of selfishness on the part of a man.   Chasing   goals   and   dreams   involves   certain commitments including time. For example, a lady wanting a degree in some field may be taking classes at a community college in the evening after her husband comes home. The husband may selfishly prefer that his wife remain home and spend time with him. This may be more common in new or younger relationships. After all, you just married her so you both could be together, and she goes running off to pursue a degree at night. If the man truly loves his woman, this will be a sacrifice he will gladly make not only to keep peace and to prevent resentment, but to see her completely fulfilled. A husband does not want to be the blame or the scapegoat for a woman who is not allowed to succeed outside of the home.

Another possible issue may involve a man's jealousy. It is not uncommon for a man to have a job he enjoys that may be deemed less prestigious than the vocation his wife pursues. If he drives a bus for instance and she wants to be an attorney, some men may feel intimidated or even pressured to change careers in some blind attempt to compete. This is merely an egotistical response and should have no play in a successful relationship. A man should feel a sense of pride and accomplishment if he is helping to support or fund the efforts of his wife, because in the long run he will be a benefactor of her success. On the contrary should he decide to fight against her ambition outside of the home, he may be left behind when she finally reaches her goal, as she will hold him in contempt for his lack of support. Being alone on holidays that were previously shared together sucks-trust me on this.

And still another issue a very few men may have with successful women is a tightly held albeit archaic viewpoint that a woman's place is in the home. I shudder to think there are still those false biases in today's world. If heaven forbid, you are one of those men, you need more help than this book will offer. If you believe the Biblical narrative, woman was made from man to be his partner and his equal, not a subservient mate with a limit on her personal dreams. Men who keep their wives down because they feel a sense of power or authority over them have completely lost touch with what it means to be a husband who cherishes his wife. A loving husband will see and recognize the dreams and goals of his wife and enable her and assist her in achieving them.

I would be less than honest if I didn't suggest that there is always a risk involved whenever you allow your wife to fly, if not risk, most certainly sacrifice. Speaking from experience, when a woman starts to successfully climb the corporate ladder, the hours at work get longer, the extracurricular meetings become more frequent, stress becomes elevated, the few hours spent at home are used to recharge and there may be little energy or time left during the week for her husband. The best advice I can give based on how poorly I mishandled it is to be above all things, patient, understanding that her lack of energy is genuine and that it is not a reflection or barometer of her feelings for you. It is also in these instances that switching roles comes into play. If you are the first one to arrive home men, plan and prepare a meal. Nothing says love more than a career woman coming home to a cooked meal by a loving husband. These are the instances to draw her a bath with music and candles for some quiet time while you tend to the kids or clean the kitchen. These are the times to have her coffee programmed and brewing when she wakes in the morning. These investments of caring and time will not go unnoticed and will pay rich dividends down the road, even though your acts should not be motivated by what's coming back to you.

Allowing your wife the freedom and the tools to fly, to chase dreams, to pursue careers and find her identity outside of the home shows her that you are a mature, loving husband invested in your relationship and her success. This is what marriage is made of. Being the wind beneath the wings of a woman you are allowing and enabling to fly may sound like a most corny cliché or an old song, but the reality is there will be a sense of pride and mutual accomplishment when you are partially responsible for the eventual success of your wife being all she wants to be.

10. Learning How and When

To Fight

When I was a younger teen I was a bit tall for my age, and not in the least bit lanky. However, it was not uncommon for others to challenge me or test me to see what I was made of. I hated this because I was not raised to be a fighter but was given full support to defend myself in any situation. I learned pretty quick that if I were to survive those schoolyard scraps I would have to throw a punch or two. Luckily for me it only took a punch or two strategically landed to end any serious confrontation.

But that mentality, not wanting to fight and avoiding confrontation at all cost has not served me well as an adult, more specifically as a husband. Knowing the monster that lies hidden deep within me I strive to be a peacemaker. To quote a fictional giant green Marvel character, you wouldn't like me when I'm angry.

Whenever we would have any serious disagreements that had the potential to escalate to a level of increased volume and elevated blood pressure, I simply clammed up, or left altogether. In my mind I was doing her a favor by not exposing her to something I was afraid might surface, but the truth is I was creating levels and layers of resentment that became the eventual cancer that killed my marriage. I had no idea at the time and would never have believed it if someone would have warned me that not fighting with my wife would cost me a twenty-year marital relationship. By the time I realized how bad it was it was too late to try to fix it. The damage was done. It wasn't sex or finances or boredom that doomed our marriage. It was simply me not knowing how and when to fight and how critical it was to resolve conflicts opposed to leaving them unresolved.

Unfortunately, I can't go back and ask for rematches like a boxer or UFC fighter. So, all I can do now is try to impress upon you the reader the importance of knowing how to fight with your spouse lest you end up in the same miserable situation I'm in now. With that I will touch on some key elements in having a loving knock-down fight with your wife-the rules, if you will. PLEASE, please, men, I beg you to understand how important this is and to take good notes.

When two people share lives and living quarters, no matter how infatuated you were with each other, there will be those times when the two of you simply don't see eye to eye on important issues. My biggest mistake was taking it personally, as if her disagreeing with me was somehow a personal rejection of me. Taking disagreements with your wife as personal attacks is your number one biggest mistake because it immediately puts you on the defense and you've already lost the battle. Fighting the correct way is in fact healthy for a relationship. Knowing that the two of you can come together and hammer out resolutions on issues you take opposite sides on gives a sense of confidence that there will be little you will encounter that together you cannot easily resolve. There's an old Proverb that says you shouldn't allow the sun to go down on unresolved anger. No truer words could have been spoken, or applied to my situation.

When two people fight there is a tendency to use the "anything goes" approach, which can unleash words that can never be retrieved once spoken. Words are important in conflict resolution.

One of the biggest ways words can hurt is when used as labels, specifically name-calling. "Words will never harm me..."-that's a lie. We use labels all the time in today's world. If someone has an opposing political view, then they must be right-wingers or communists. If someone was raised differently than you were they might be rednecks or thugs. We use labels so easily we don't even realize it and they can be very polarizing. But when used in marriage they can be cancerous. If in the heat of the battle you tell your wife she's being psycho, neurotic, schizoid, etc., you've done her a great disservice. First, labels reduce her to commonality and rob her of any uniqueness. Saying something like "you're as crazy as all other chics" or something similar groups her with ordinary women you don't even know. She will hear instead, I don't love you anymore than the woman down the street. It's mean, vicious and solves nothing. It DOES, however, create a barrier between you that will take much effort and time to tear down.

Labels can be much milder but have the same effect. "You're being silly", "you're such a bore", "why are you so depressing", all just as damaging. Women need to her words of confirmation even in a good fight. When you resort to name-calling, it shows first, you haven't developed the tools and skills required to engage in verbal battle. Second, it will cause your wife to call into question every positive confirmation you have given her, if you can so easily toss them aside and reduce her to a label. Labels are used to reveal what's inside a given product. They will also reveal to your wife just what is inside of you.

Another unfair weapon in confrontation is the use of history. Even courts of law exclude legal arguments from previous cases not relevant to the case at hand because they deem it to have little or no bearing on the verdict. Yet couple use this tactic quite often when fighting. Unfortunately, we don't have the luxury of a defense attorney to "Object" as Irrelevant on our behalf. It's really important to know what is categorized as history in confrontations so we are not guilty of unfairly using it.

If you are alive and breathing, you have screwed up along the way, even in your relationship. And if you've been married any amount of time, you will most likely have a trail of mistakes that are in your past. Your significant other will as well. And that is precisely where they need to remain. If, in the midst of an exchange you say something like "you never have done this or that" or "it's always the same thing with you", those are implied historic positions that should not be a present consideration. Statements can also be much more direct, such as "remember that time when you (fill in the blank)" or "I still can't get over when you...". The problem we have with certain things in the past is this-we can't remember what we ate for breakfast yesterday, but we will never forget when someone hurt us. We have the capacity to forgive, but the forgetting part is a challenge. When wrongs have been confessed and forgiven in a relationship they need to remain buried in the past. But for many past hurt is a defense mechanism because they never really got over the grievance and it lies just beneath the surface for easy access as a weapon for the next battle. This just shouldn't be. Men, we will certainly have more wrongs for our wives to dig up.

My ex-wife used this tactic unfairly on me. We disagreed on certain parenting methods, not that one was more right than the other, just different styles due to upbringing. And yet even after our adult children were grown and out of the home, I would still be reminded of how I should have done this or that differently when they were still living at home. This use of history automatically put me in a defensive posture and became a smoke screen to the issue at hand, resulting in little to no real resolution of any significance. Bringing up the past hurts during a confrontation will always yield ZERO results.

Another rule for fair fighting involves volume. There are times when volume is a great thing-at a concert of your favorite band, in the stadium watching a sporting event, or cheering on your kids during athletic competition. And there are times when volume is detrimental. One of those times would be during a confrontation. When we get heated up it is natural to inflect volume into our speech. Shouting matches are never won simply by being the loudest. We can get our points and concerns across with change of tone, exaggerated pronunciation or hand gestures, but raising the voice is simply another smoke screen designed as a defensive strategy that achieves nothing in the process of confrontation.   Make eye contact, speak clearly and deliberately and use inflection so as not to be monotone, but keep the volume under control.

Formulating a defense while your partner is still speaking is another unfair fighting tactic. I was guilty of this a lot. As soon as I knew what we were fighting about, I stopped listening to all the reasons my wife was upset and instead was formulating in my mind some type of a defense or comeback.   This never works, especially if there is something specific, and there usually is, that you have done to upset your mate. If she is fighting fair and is relaying to you properly the issue and why it's a concern to her, yours is to remain silent and humble and allow her the courtesy of completing her train of thought, careful not to miss anything important because you are scouring your mental notes like a good defense attorney waiting to cross-examine. Men can't resolve conflicts if they don't know entirely what the conflict is.   Conflicts can only be identified and acknowledged through attentive listening skills.   In addition, it's highly important to hear what she ISN'T saying as this too is a clue to just how concerned she is with the topic at hand. Again, this is impossible to do if you aren't hearing her every word.

Embellishment or exaggeration is yet another tool of an unfair fighter. We use exaggeration a million times a day (see?) without realizing it. It can be harmless enough when chatting with friends. "He must have jumped a mile high" or "I flew out of there at 100 miles per hour", just used to make points, no harm and completely understood as exaggerations. However, when used in the course of verbal confrontation, they immediately convey a lack of credible arguing skills and put the other on defense.

"Honey, I've asked you a thousand times…"

"You are always late"

"You never help around the house"

"I swear your brain is the size of a pea"

"You never listen"

"I wish I'd never met you"

…and so on.

When you resort to blowing things out of proportion, or *making mountains out of mole hills,* the heart of the issue gets lost and yet again, nothing is settled. Don't dismiss the argument by using exaggerations that unfairly characterize your wife. That my work with boxers tying to hype up ticket sales for a major fight but it will yield no results in coming to solutions with your wife.

The last thing I would add to this list of the rules of engagement is this-CONFLICT RESOLUTION IS NOW ABOUT WINNING AN ARGUMENT! Most men I know have a competitive streak or nature in them. Whether you are golfing with a buddy or playing poker with the boys (or ladies) on the weekend, we all have a tendency to win and even get a little bit disgruntled when we don't. I remember when I played basketball in school I would take defeat hard and it was normal for me to shoulder the blame even if I had a good game. I don't like losing to anyone, except maybe my grandkids. But conflicts in a marriage are not opportunities to improve your fighting record. If you come into a marital argument with a 24-0 record, something has gone terribly wrong and even though you think you have a winning record, you may have already lost the war and just haven't been informed yet!

Note we are not referring to common bickering over leaving the toilet seat up or forgetting to buy milk-we are addressing those things that your wife feels strongly enough about that she has brought it to your attention, one way or another and whatever it is needs to be resolved. In this spirit you don't load up or grab a few extra rounds or clips from your arsenal, ready for an all-out assault. Marriage is not a TV game show-when it comes to a healthy fight with our mate we are not *in it to win it*. Quite the opposite must be true if progress is to be made that yields understanding, compromise if called for, and eventual mutually beneficial resolution. Knowing how and when to fight with your wife, applying the fair rules of engagement as we've laid out, and understanding the importance of not letting unresolved issues simmer beneath the surface as if they have been laid to rest when in fact they are simply hibernating ready to come alive again under the right set of circumstances-these factors all guarantee a win-win situation for both man and wife. In marriage the worst fight is the one that never takes place! The best fight is the one in which both parties walk away feeling like they've been heard, their concerns mattered to their partner and the result was a loving draw.

11. The Other Three Words She Needs to Hear

By now, and especially after the previous chapter, you may think that I am painting a loving and considerate husband or partner as a mindless, spineless, wimpy shell of a male whose man card has been permanently revoked. Of course, that would be a gross misconception. Above all things I believe a woman wants to be with a strong man. But, by definition, men make mistakes, especially when it comes to women. And when they occur, I humble spirit and a contrite heart will go a long way in patching things up with your mate. In that light, it is very important that men are open and willing to tell their wives these three tiny but powerful words.... *I Am Sorry!*

The word *sorry* means to be remorseful, repentant, or regretful. It implies the notion that you did something that you may or may not have known would result in harm or ill feelings, and that it was not your intent to do so. We've already discussed thee numerous ways we men can upset our women, so it only follows that having a remorseful heart will serve us well and please our wives. However, those three words may be as foreign to a man's tongue as *"why yes, I have enough shoes"* would be to a woman's. Groveling doesn't come across as a very manly trait. Buy being sorry, saying that you are sorry and showing her that you in fact are sorry are musts for couples who desire a long-term marriage and milestone anniversaries.

When a man is faced with challenge that an apology is in order, it is always easiest and the best policy to address it quickly and not put it off for ANY amount of time. More than likely by the time you realize that you need to apologize for something, your wife has already figured this out and has been waiting to hear and see those magic words. Don't procrastinate, get it done.

Be sincere. There is little worse than an insincere apology. I recall vividly whenever my little brother and I would fight over something, our father would demand that we tell the other that we were sorry. I'm sure you are familiar with the scene and how it plays out. We were forced to utter the words, but it was apparent to all that it was just a ritualistic exercise that had little believability. We were so sorry we might not speak to each other for days before we eventually became *truly* sorry. But our mates are not our siblings-they can spot a phony apology a mile away (ah, an exaggeration). Why men still think they can get things over on their women is beyond me. It never worked on my mom or my grandmother-it most certainly will not work with a wife. Sincerity is a virtue, a *chivalrous* virtue that women expect and deserve.

Apologies need to be *empathetic*. In other words, it is highly important for both you and your spouse to have a full understanding of why the actions or lack of in question caused harm or pain. Men this goes right along with knowing your wife, what makes her tick, what sets her off, what things she may be sensitive to, etc. Major corporations and agencies employ sensitivity training for their workers to help them be aware of those they work with or work for. Perhaps marriage classes should include a course on sensitivity. Knowing your wife's hot buttons is not something that will happen right after wedding vows, but the longer you are married and the more you learn about the other, the more aware you will become of those things that are you mate's Achilles heel. Is she over conscious about her figure? Did she flunk her cooking classes? Does she have a unique laugh? Joking about things like this even in a loving manner are bound to cause hurt feelings. Once you can fully understand how your actions made your wife feel and why, you will be less likely to make the same misjudgments in the future.

Show true *remorse*. Remorse is a deep regret or feeling of guilt for an action or wrong that was committed. Every year hundreds of inmates incarcerated for crimes they committed and serving the subsequent sentence for that crime, become eligible to be paroled after serving a required minimum amount of time as handed down by the judge. We just had a rather famous inmate be paroled here in the State of NV in a proceeding aired nationally on television and internet. It was made clear that one of the most important factors the parole board looks for is whether or not the perspective parolee shows any remorse for their crime. Remorse carries much weight. It is one thing to say how sorry you are and quite another to show deep regret for your actions, wishing you could take it back or change the outcome. This is a very real and transparent response for any woman to perceive. Remorse is taking sorry to a more genuine level, one that if done properly will cause your wife to be open, responsive and forgiving, which leads to the next action point.

Ask for forgiveness. If there is anything more difficult than uttering the words "I am sorry", it's following them up with "please forgive me". Asking for forgiveness puts men in an uncomfortable and vulnerable state. We are literally throwing ourselves on the marital judgment bench and asking for mercy from our wives. Forgiveness after conflicts is essential for both parties. For the offender, it serves as a reprieve-a lighter sentence for good behavior if you will. It acknowledges that something happened that needed to be forgiven and mercy was granted. For the defendant, it is a must in order to move forward. It is not practical in marriage to employ forgive and forget. Our minds are like steel traps when we've been hurt. We must always be capable and willing to forgive our spouses, fully, unconditionally and without prejudice, meaning in legal terms, the case can't be reopened at a later date for the same offense. For those of us of the faith, there is a term used that describes how our sin is forgiven and removed from us as far as the east is from the west. It's a great notion in marital forgiveness. When men ask for forgiveness it should mean that you have adequately discussed and reconciled the grievance and you want to move forward with said offense wiped from the record. An unforgiven reconciliation is not a reconciliation-it's an agreement to disagree. Be sure your wife is satisfied that whatever caused the conflict has been fully addressed and resolved by her granting your request for forgiveness.

An old rocker wrote a song entitled *Sorry Seems to be the Hardest Word.* It doesn't have to be that way!

12. *Be an Engaged Father to*

Your Children

I wasn't completely sure if I should include this chapter or not. On the surface fatherhood seems to be an entirely different issue with a different set of skills and challenges worthy of the many How-To books written on the subject. But upon deeper reflection I determined that many of the qualities necessary to be a good dad are very similar to the qualities needed to be a good husband, traits recognized and loved by women. Some of the most endearing images shared by women as being sexy are images of a manly man tenderly holding a baby in his arms. The fatherly show of love coupled with the resolve to protect his child against any and all threats, is attractive and comforting to a woman.

I am not convinced there is any such thing as paternal instincts, at least not initially. Mothers carry this child in their womb for nine months, grow loving bonds, have a real physical connection, and at birth, merely express an external love based on a nine-month connection of nurturing and internal love. They became a mother the moment they realized they conceived! Dads on the other hand, are on the outside looking in. Say what you will about being there through false labor pains, midnight runs to the store for wild food cravings, mood swings and all that goes along with the mom's body changing, it is simply not the same thing for men. Our anticipation and desire to be a parent does not equate to the none-month head start and bond between the mom and the child. Therefore, we become instant students in an on-the-job training that comes quickly and naturally to some, but not for all. We must learn how to be protective, loving, guiding and selfless when it comes to fatherhood. It should be no surprise that the better dads make the better husbands.

Women like their men to be playful or have a fun side.

Nothing brings out the kid in a man more than playing with his own children, or for some of us, grandchildren. This is easy for most men because quite frankly, we never really grow up inside and fatherhood gives us an excuse to let the boy in us come out. As I give examples from my own experience in this chapter I in no form or fashion promote myself as a model father. I was far from it, adequate at best compared to my own father, but I tried. I remember how much fun I had with my boys when they were younger. The times were of course simpler and much more meaningful. Little things like wrestling with them on the floor, usually all at the same time, or playing games with them. They loved amusement parks and the kiddie rides in Old Indiana and what used to be called Santa Claus Land. Even as they grew into older teens my wife still got a kick out of seeing us all on the rollercoaster or whatever the latest crazy thrill ride of the day may be. There was/is little I won't ride with them to this day. My oldest son, now in his mid-thirties, still has as his mission to experience every major rollercoaster in the country, and has passed that love of the thrill onto his son, my grandson. As important as it is to have fun with your children, it is equally important that your spouse witness the interaction you have with your kids. It gives her a level of deeper respect and admiration for you as dad, and as her playful, young-at-heart mate.

Women want and need their men to be protectors and defenders.

Our children need to know that their dad always has their back and will do anything necessary to defend and protect them from any danger, up to and including risking life and limb to keep them from harm. Growing up in the Midwest and raising kids in the eighties, there was not much in the way of danger as far as any criminal element was concerned. Sure, there were always the usual schoolyard scraps but nothing too serious or challenging. Moving from Indiana to Las Vegas, however, presented an entirely foreign set of challenges and cultural changes that presented opportunities for bad things to happen if you were not paying attention. I recall an incident in our first apartment when I learned of a group of young males distributing drugs in our complex and, without thinking, I ran out the door and chased them out of the parking lot. At least one of them fired off a round at me. I wasn't about to allow strangers to introduce my boys to narcotics and was willing to get dirty to make sure it didn't happen. This response is seen by a wife as a superman trait that gives her the same reassurance that you would do the same to protect her.

The protection doesn't have to be always so dramatic. It could be a neighborhood kid bullying your child or an over-zealous coach belittling them during a game. It might be the daily things like not starting the car until they are buckled in or being on time to pick them up from school. Whatever the case your children are watching much more closely than you realize, to be affirmed in their own minds that you are a dependable protector, and your wife is watching too!

Women want men who are true to their convictions.

Of all the responsibilities of fatherhood, I always hated and found it extremely unfair that discipline fell on the shoulders of the dad. It never seemed equitable to me that moms get the loving stuff, but dads have to play the bad cop whenever the child steps out of line. The old "wait til your father gets home" attitude always caused a bit of resentment in me, even though I realized from experience the horror a child goes through in the hours he or she has to wait or what's coming when dad gets home and mom spills the beans.

And yet loving discipline, guidance, correction and sound moral teachings are all fundamental tenets for any dad who gives a damn about his children. It simply boils down to the fact that if you don't train them properly, someone else will train them improperly! We live in a world now where a parent's hands are tied somewhat by the courts and Child Protective Services. As a result, many dads are afraid to get in the faces of their children when they need and want it most! Our kids will never ask for the consequences of bad decisions, but they will appreciate it after the lesson and values are taught. In virtually every culture going back to ancient times, it is the responsibility of the father to "train up a child in the way he or she should go", to quote a Biblical passage. We are to make sure they understand manners by the way they see us treat and love on their moms. They are to understand the importance of education by our involvement with parent/teacher conferences when the opportunity arises. If you are of the faith, it is your responsibility to expose them to the foundation of your beliefs, so they can make intelligent choices at the proper time. It is your job to see and recognize talents and skills and to help them develop and hone them into vocational or professional career aspirations. These all fall under the umbrella of discipline, guidance and training, a man's responsibility. Many will be the times that your wife will desire your input or guidance for some important decision she needs to make, and seeing how you handle your job as a father will confirm in her mind your ability to guide her when requested as well. Who knows, she may even ask for some discipline from you herself when feeling the urge.

Women want their men to show pride in them.

When it comes to our children, parents are the first to show pride in their achievements, accomplishments and efforts. There is nothing that says fatherhood more than a dad proud of his children, even if just for being his children. I learned much about this from my own father. After the sixth grade I was always involved in school athletics of some kind, specifically basketball and track. My dad worked a factory job and didn't clock out until three PM. He made every effort to be present at all my games or events. I can't recall any he missed. If it were a basketball game he would be there in the stands encouraging the whole team, yelling when we scored and harping on the refs for missed or bad calls. If it were a track meet I knew that when I rounded the corner from a running lap his voice would be the one I would hear above the crowd and his face would be the first I saw clinging to the fence as close as he could get to the track to cheer me on to the finish line. I never had any doubt in all my childhood that my dad was proud of me, and I am saddened when I hear of kids who never knew of such staunch support from their fathers.

When I had boys of my own and times were rough, I missed out on many similar opportunities to be there because I was working two jobs to support them. The choice between providing necessities and going to events is a terrible choice because either way, a dad loses. I failed at achieving the same level of support for them that my dad showed me. I am trying to make it up now with both them and my grandchildren. Moments can never be recaptured once wasted. Measure accurately the eternal benefits of your time management when it comes to being there for your children. When a woman sees the sense of pride a father shows for his children she is assured that he is just as boastful and appreciative of her and will be her biggest fan in all her endeavors as well.

Women want a man who can show humility, vulnerability and meekness.

Meekness is often confused with wimpiness, not the case at all. Meekness is defined as strength restrained or controlled. I often referred to my own father as a gentle giant. With a 6'8" frame and weight in at 300 lbs., he had a heart of gold and a gentle spirit. The softer edges of fatherhood are important in the lives of their children.

Knowing how to relate to them at whatever age level they are at shows a willingness to put aside the maturity of the man

103

so that the meekness of the child can come out and bond with sons and daughters. It takes a humble and playful attitude to allow your daughter or granddaughter put make up on you or braid your hair. It takes humility to play tea time or dress up with a girl who looks to you as her hero. It takes vulnerability to tell your son you are sorry and that you made a mistake. Each of these traits, humility, vulnerability and meekness are just as applicable in a marriage relationship. It's great to be the knight on the horse, but there will be times that call for you to dismount and remove your armor and leave yourself unprotected with your spouse. This defenseless posture shows total trust to your wife in ways she will appreciate. She knows your strengths; she admires your meekness.

The qualities found in great fathers parlay into the makings of great husbands. In many ways the approach you take with your children will be mimicked in your approach with your wife. Dads who have great bonds and relationships with their kids also have great relationships with their wives. And sadly, dads who don't have strong fatherly bonds will show similar weak spots in their marriages. Children are a blessing born of a mutual and loving compilation. The stronger the ties between dads and their children, the stronger the bonds of their marriage.

13. You Can't Be Her Everything

"Without you I'd be nothing."

"You are my everything."

"If I have you I have everything."

"All I want for Christmas is you."

"You are my every breath."

The phrases above may make for nice greeting card verses of song titles. It's nice to think that our spouse's world revolved around us and that as long as we are around, they will be happy. But the truth is quite the opposite. While we have spent several chapters dealing with how to reconnect to each other, men and women alike need time away from their partners to develop friendships with others so that there is no social cavity in their person. The adage "a boy's night out" applies equally to the girls.

I'm no expert on the social aspects or health benefits of a woman's life outside of the home, but I have an idea or two about why men want their boys' night, so I'm going to attempt to draw some parallels, so we men can have a better understanding and appreciation of why our women need occasional nights away from us. I think we will discover that the reasons are very similar.

Men like to hang out with the boys so they can act out without the discretionary glances from their wives. They can fart, belch, make armpit noises, throw back a few brews, tell off-color jokes, all without having to answer for their behavior. It's a testosterone fest that only men can truly understand. So, the same must be true of women. A night out with other girls allows them to resort to being girls, the ones they were before marriage and/or motherhood. They can temporarily escape the duties of changing diapers, cooking meals, wiping noses-those things which they may never complain about and deep down may be overall grateful for, but still things from which it's nice to take a short break from. And who knows, they may even fart around other women!

Men like to talk to other men about things their wives may not understand or be into, e.g. sports, cars, etc. Therefore, it would follow that women need such opportunities as well. Even if you have paid attention to previous chapters about developing your conversation skills, there will always be those topics women simply share with other women, e.g. shopping, the latest in a series of novels, fashion or even just other women. Undoubtedly, they will share their marital war stories as well. If you are doing your job your lady will realize through the revelation of her friends that she has fared well in her marriage in comparison. Women gossiping about their mates could work to your benefit. Women also like to vent about their careers, children, their weight and yes, their views on social issues, especially if they are not given respectful dialogue on such with their men. If couples share opposing political views, we men all too quickly pass them off as being clueless-we can be so little and demeaning at times with our mates.

Men want to be trusted to go out with the boys without getting the third degree when they return home, even if the boys end up at bars or clubs. Even though married, we still appreciate the beauty of other women and want to feel free to express their approval of the opposite sex without retaliation or misinterpreted intent from the wives. SOOOO......Women should expect nothing less. There are so many things out there for women to do together from karaoke bars to art and canvas parties to movies to, yes-strip clubs. For all the reasons a man wants to feel trusted to look but not touch, a woman too needs similar trust and freedom to enjoys such encounters with her friends. It will most certainly benefit a man if his woman gets as visually worked up as the man does when he's around young hotties. At the end of the night you both bring it home to the one you love. But for some reason this seems to get lost on many men.

Men like to go out dressed in the fashion that is most natural and comfortable to them. For many that might be jeans and a t-shirt. They won't catch flack by other men for dressing down. Women are much the same but with opposite expressions. Women may want to dress up, get girlie, wear flats and a fun hairstyle, things they may not do when out with their husbands. Dressing up is fun for women when they don't have to, just like cooking is fun for some men when they don't have to cook every day. Playful party dresses, maybe themed outfits, crazy combos-all are things that make a woman a girl, and that girl needs to come out from time to time just like the boy in the man does.

We mentioned in the chapter on cleaning that a woman's identity many times centers around her home. But there are those times when even she needs a different perspective on her domestication, one that can only come from stepping away from it for a short time. Even as men need vacations from jobs they may absolutely love, women need a break from the constant care and maintenance of their domicile so they can return with a better appreciation and renewed vigor to tackle that which she loves. Guys should encourage their wives to get out of the house as often as necessary if it helps her to maintain her sanity from the daily responsibility of being a mom and wife, even for weekend getaways with the girls. That should need no further explanation.

There is a passage in the New Testament that says two cords are strong, but three cords are not easily broken. The reference has much to do with brother/sisterhood and the allies of friendly relationships. When you are sitting in a large house void of laughter or companionship due to a broken marriage relationship, you will have a deeper understanding of the small price of letting your mate out of the house for her own social and mental welfare, and the health of your relationship. In fact, given the obvious from studies and research, smart men should insist that their wives make girl plans regularly, even including out of town excursions, just so the woman can reclaim her identity. When you married, she more than likely took your last name and may have been completely absorbed into your identity as merely your wife. She needs to be afforded the opportunity to get in touch with the woman she was before marriage so that she can appreciate the fact that marriage did not cause her to lose herself but that it in fact helped enhance the beautiful person she always was and still is. A man cannot and should not expect to be his wife's all-in-all, because, men, you and I will usually fail at that task miserably. We need to allow other women to fulfill the social needs of our spouse so that our women are free to love us of their own will and not a sense of dependence we mistakenly created in order to promote loyalty. Loving with a free heart is always the preferred method in any relationship. When your wife is free to live, she will be free to love!

14. Important Dates-

Our Opportunity

We have all seen and laughed at TV episodes where a man is lambasted for forgetting a date held sacred to his wife, usually the all-important Anniversary date. Women are very sentimental about the tiniest of events that were meaningful to them. They may easily recall their first kiss, their very first date, things that happened in their school years-events that most men couldn't recollect if their lives depended on it. Women also attach significant feelings of endearment to such episodes, much more so than most of us men do, like the weed pressed between the pages of the scrapbook. And yet the thought that an important event in the couple's past may be significant enough that the man would indeed commemorate it with some thoughtful gesture is enough to make up for a year's worth of uh-ohs and apologies with the wifey. Needless to say, men need to schedule in their calendars the all-important opportunities to remember certain significant days. With today's virtual calendars, now even available to wear on your wrist, there should be no excuse to miss the important dates and those you've penciled in around them.

It is not that a man can't remember such events. We can tell you who won Super Bowl 25 and who the MVP was and whether your team covered the point spread or not. Some might remember the first time they tore into a carburetor just to put it back together again. Others might recall the very first fish they hooked or the girl to whom we lost our virginity. What appears to be different in men and women is not the capacity to recall to memory but rather the significance we assign differently to certain events. Without relinquishing the memories of those things we men hold near and dear, it is vital, in as much as it is possible, to understand how differently the female mind and heart processes moments of importance so that through that understanding we are more compelled to join her in recalling and celebrating the events that make up your history as a couple. These are opportunities for you to reaffirm your love and her importance in your life. They unfortunately are also road hazards if you let them slip by without any acknowledgment!

There are always the most obvious of dates, those that if you are dumb enough to forget, you may as well get a room for all the loving reception you won't receive when you walk through the door empty-handed. We shouldn't have to list them but assuming nothing on my part, let's be clear lest you commit unforgivable event omissions!

The king of all dates, the **Wedding Anniversary**.

This should be important, it is the day the two of you officially became one single family unit on a road of mutual love and commitment to the other. Of all the unpardonable sins with a couple, forgetting the day you married ranks up there with sleeping with her best friend-it is that important! We always had a special place where we enjoyed dinner in Laguna Beach, even if it wasn't on our actual anniversary date. We set it aside on our annual vacations as a time to remember, and it quickly became a tradition. With couples who both work outside of the home it may be difficult to have a special night out if the date falls somewhere in the middle of the week, but even if plans are made to celebrate come the weekend, a card, a token-something is appropriate for the actual date itself.

Traditionally there are certain gifts and even gemstones you give to mark certain anniversaries. For example, Silver commemorates twenty-five years and gold commemorates fifty years. But there are actually similar suggestions for each of the years. Men would so impress their wives if they knew and presented gifts that coincided with a specific year. Example, for a fifth anniversary the modern gift is silverware and the gemstone is sapphire, while the suggested colors are blue, pink and turquoise. Any gift that incorporated these suggestions with items you know your wife is into, will look really good for you. The eighth year is linen or lace and the color, bronze. Use your imagination to her delight. Of all days on the calendar year be sure that she is fondly remembered and celebrated on your Wedding Anniversary date.

Another obvious day to remember is **her birthday**.

Need I stress how important it is to not only remember her birthday but to know how old she is? Birthday celebrations are great because it gives the whole family and circle of friends an opportunity to hang out and have fun. And, like anniversaries, there will be those milestone birthdays the two of you celebrate as you grow old together-turning thirty, forty, fifty and so on. These are the birthdays when you can introduce some brevity into the celebration, nothing overboard but all in fun as you show gratitude for another blessed year of life and love. Surprise parties are extremely difficult to pull off on women because, let's face it, she's expecting you to do something special. So, the only surprise element will be how you pull it off, not IF you pull it off. So be creative, imaginative and ask for help if necessary but make it memorable.

I'm not sure if I could speak for women but I would hazard a guess that the next most important date to remember is **Valentine's Day.**

If you are in your fifties or sixties you most likely went to a school that hosted Valentine parties and allowed a time to exchange Valentines with class members, so that even in our informative years the significance of this love holiday was ingrained into us. For the most part, females never grow out of it and why would they. Everyone from Hallmark to Hollywood to Hershey's has jumped on the holiday revenue train in a concerted marketing effort to exploit consumer guilt spending for every penny. Even some churches acknowledge the day as an opportunity to offer dinners or candlelight events focused on couples and their relationships. But for the informed man, this is not a guilt-driven date but rather the perfect opportunity to shower your gal with flowers, chocolate, lace or whatever else you come up with to show her once again how much she means and the important role she plays in your life. It's also the perfect chance for you to be playful in your approach. Valentine cards rarely say exactly what you would say if you were writing them. Apparently, you don't need to be much of a word crafter to be employed as a Hallmark verse writer. If you are like me, you may find greeting cards woefully inadequate or expressive, even for a man. So why not slip a little something extra in the card from your own thoughts

113

and words. It could be as simple as a heartfelt I Love You to a playful ode from your vast wit.

I love writing limericks because they are so easy to compose but always so well received, even or especially when suggestive in nature. It could be as simple as this:

The poems of love have been read

The words from the heart have been said

When we're done for the night

Let's turn down all the lights

And continue the romance in bed.

Women go absolutely gaga over silly but creative odes like this. Learn how to form these simple rhymes and find excuses to present your lover with them often, whether it's an important date to remember or just because it's Tuesday.

Next on the date-to-remember list would probably be **Mother's Day**.

If your wife is also a mother, she needs double attention on this special day. While it's the obvious occasion for children to shower their moms with love and appreciation, the role of motherhood is just one more thing that should endear her to her husband, and another chance for him to show his love, respect and honor for the timeless and often thankless role of being a mom. Children are a blessing and they are the living, breathing result of the two becoming one and seeing something miraculous happen as a result!

Dads don't always embrace the role of a parent as he should, or at least I know I didn't. As mentioned earlier, the normal physical bond between a mother and the child she carries in her for nine months is something special and quite unique in comparison the that of the man through the pregnancy. Naturally it would be difficult for even the best fathers to fully grasp the bond between mother and child, but that bond is obvious to all who see her and cause for celebration and acknowledgment. The best thing a man can do for his wife on Mother's Day is to see to it that she has to do absolutely nothing but show up!

The traditional holidays of **Easter, Thanksgiving and Christmas** are also holidays that should not go by without acknowledgment as they too are great opportunities to express your love and appreciation for your wife. The accompanying sentiments of love and gratitude for these holidays should never be lost on your mate. Letting her know that above all you are thankful to have her as your wife on Thanksgiving will simply reassure her that she is foremost on your mind. And to have no greater gift on Christmas than her love as your wife will certainly get you year off to a great start.

There are also those secondary of St. Patrick's Day, Halloween, a fun Cinco de Mayo or any other lesser celebrated days when a casual lunch or romantic dinner with green beer or spooky drink concoctions can be fun and appreciated. The idea is to never let a holiday go by without you seeing the opportunity to shower your spouse with attention, just as you would have in the dating phase. It helps keep a marriage fresh and exciting. The only bad days to celebrate are the ones you forget about!

15. Overlooking Those Little Things

You've been looking for your dream home for quite a while now. You may not have been exactly sure what it would look like but you had definite ideas about what features you wanted it to have in order for you to feel comfortable in your new space. The realtor shows you a new listing that just arrived on the market. Your first impression was favorable, but you needed to see more. As you make your way through the home you are pleasantly surprised that it has everything on your list and you can't wait to make an offer. That day finally arrives, the day you close and get the keys to your new home.

You move in and life is beautiful, at first. But with time you begin to notice little things that you missed on the initial inspection. A couple of the tiles in the kitchen have small cracks in them that have obviously been repaired. Some of the base boards in the living room have chips in the paint. One of the lights in the entry way chandelier is missing and another one isn't working. One of the bathroom faucets has a very slow drip. Soon you realize that your dream home has flaws-nothing major or irreparable, but as you compose your list you lose sight of the overall beauty and charm of your home because your focus is on a list of things that are less than perfect, and you develop buyer's remorse. Nothing changed after you moved in-those little flaws were always there, you just overlooked them in your zeal to acquire the home before someone else snatched it off the market because deep down you knew it was the perfect home for you.

And such is marriage!

You didn't know what she would look like but you knew what characteristics, what traits she would need to have for you to feel compatible with her, and when you finally met her and knew you needed to see more, she was everything you dreamed of and more. She met all your criteria. You had to have her, you proposed to her, closed escrow and made her your wife. Life was grand, at first. But with time you began to notice the little things that in your zeal you had overlooked before. Or, you might have noticed them, but the reward outweighed the list of issues and you dismissed it.

Up until now we have been singing the praises of our wives and creating a case for how we need to love, honor, cherish and protect our treasure to ensure a happy marriage. But the fact is that only One, has ever walked this planet as perfect. All of us have issues, flaws, habits, little traits, that in a new relationship, are often overlooked. But as we spend real time together, experiencing every day work and living together, we are bound to be made aware of things we dismissed as newlyweds. This is definitely true of men, and most likely true of our women. It could be minute in nature. Maybe she insists on running a half-full dishwasher. Perhaps she has a routine of facial treatment before going to bed that has an odor that disagrees with your senses. Maybe she runs the gas tank in the car to a level lower than you would ever dare. Or maybe those noises she makes during sex that you thought were cute at first now bother you a bit for some strange reason, opposed to the alternative of being with someone who lays motionless and quiet. Whatever the case, this dream person you fell for hasn't changed, but now your focus is on the list, not the person. The flaws which were never a consideration at the onset of your relationship are now grabbing your attention like flashing lights.

There is a wise scripture which reads "Love doesn't keep track of wrongs", that is to say, love doesn't keep a list. Wise counsel indeed. At issue in most cases is simply a change in perception. When considering the dream home, you were looking at all the features that made you want to close the deal, and not reasons to walk away and keep looking. Likewise, in marriage you were focused on the whole person and everything she meant to you and all the things that were attractive to you, and not the flaws that would cause you to break things off. What you willingly choose to focus on will become a false reality. The deception of perception will kill an otherwise healthy relationship.

Whenever someone has beauty, talent, worth as a whole, but they are increasingly viewed and graded, not through the former wide-angle lens, but now a microscope, they unfairly become the sum of their imperfections. When a man stops seeing all the accumulative value and worth of the whole of his wife and begins to zoom in on the little things to the point that the whole is reduced to a few insignificant flaws, that man may never be able again to see her as he once did. The wife never changed in the least-only the perception of her husband did. What we fail to consider is that the wife has the same zoom capability as we do, should she resort to

118

using it on us, and the results would be much the same. Our overall value would be viewed microscopically, and our flaws would be highlighted so as to be defined solely by our imperfections. How sad when this is allowed to happen!

How can men recognize and avoid this trap as soon as it becomes apparent? Perhaps one of the greatest defenses against perception issues is to put into practice all we discussed earlier about the importance of continual dating, the constant reminders of why we fell for her in the first place. I can tell you at least I know that the tricks work. In twenty years of marriage both I and my wife aged considerably, and our youthful appearance changed with time. And yet I never stopped seeing in her the younger version of her that I first fell in love with, not simply the physical appearance but all those traits that snared me from the beginning, the laugh, the smile, the flirt, the eyes. Whatever happens in my future life, I will never forget the first time I looked into those beautiful sea blue eyes because through the years I never stopped looking into them and the image in my mind is indelible. That practice will work when you begin to see something you question. Just change your view and make a choice to see something else that you still find loving and compelling.

We all have power over the thoughts and images that invade our mind. We are our own safety filter. We can allow what gets through, what gets filtered, what is quickly dismissed and what we choose to dwell on. It is not involuntary-it is a matter of our will and desire. We can choose to take captive any negative thought and dismiss it as incidental. If you are seeing things you dismissed earlier, it may be a sign that there is something looming that is larger than the cracked tile you suddenly noticed. It is something that you need to stop and diagnose so you can refocus on the larger picture.

While we spent two chapters discussing the importance of honest conversation, these little nuances that you are suddenly aware of are not necessarily a subject you should bring up over dinner. When you begin to tell a woman about things you don't find appealing, they react in a most negative way. They will take something you said in passing and over-analyze it until it becomes an even bigger flaw to her than it was to you. This kind of brutal honesty is a death warrant for her esteem, and quite possibly your marriage. This is true especially for those things that are really of no significance, but that you yourself have blown out of proportion as a result of your magnification. Please find some way to make these suddenly noticeable issues fade once again into the bigger picture. No one is perfect in every way, but two people can be entirely perfect together when you as the husband train yourself how to overlook the little things.

16. SEX!

Foreplay Begins in the Kitchen

By now you are probably wondering if I was ever going to get to the chapter on sex. If so, you have already missed the point of all the previous chapters. Everything we have covered to this point has been about intimacy. It's just that for many men, the very word *intimacy* conjures up thought of physical contact, heavy breathing and a sweaty sprint to the finish. But for women sex encompasses all the above, the dating, the quiet moments, the subtle affections, the tokens of appreciation, the helping out around the house-all those things that light her fire without you even realizing it, not just the few moments at the end of the day in bed or on the surface of your choice. All these things keep her engine idling, if you will, so that when the time comes for that which you consider intimacy, you will not be starting an engine that hasn't been running for a few days and waiting for it to warm up, but rather you will simply be putting into gear that which has been running all along and is ready for a ride.

This will not be a Masters and Johnson type chapter on sexual techniques, the highway of nerves that course their way through the female anatomy or a Cosmopolitan lecture on how to drive your woman wild in bed, as I stated in the

Introduction. I have to defer those topics to the true experts. I won't presume to know everything about sending your wife into spasms of orgasms-I doubt any man truly knows all there is to know about female sexuality. But what I hope it *will* be is a how-to for men on the overall approach to physical intimacy, the things your mama didn't teach you, the things you will undoubtedly will never learn in your local church or parish, including loving aspirations, realistic goals and hopefully, orgasmic results.

I will attempt to make some observations that some men may overlook in their approach to sex. We men are often described as having two heads, with the smaller one exercising authority over the larger one. Not sure if I can totally disagree with that description. God only knows how many times men have gotten themselves into trouble by letting an erection determine their direction. Mating is certainly one of man's primal and basic instincts, but even the most unstoppable of forces can be intensified when properly controlled. We can't be justified for our indiscretions simply because we are men and that's just what men do! What a cowardly copout to chivalrous and gentlemanly behavior. Our wives deserve our absolute and total sexual interest and passion and pent up energy so that she can be a reciprocal participant in the God-designed euphoric pleasure that is sex.

Many sex researchers agree that the most vital of all sex organs for men is not the penis but the brain. I can hear 95% of readers closing the book in disagreement, but the truth is they are correct. There are the noted discoveries about the brain and sex which are well documented and not disputed. For example, the neurotransmitters that released during physical arousal are the same ones released during a chemical high. In that case I guess you can say Robert palmer was right when he wrote the popular hit, *Addicted to Love*. There is also the fact that the part of the brain that controls the mating instinct in men is nearly twice the size of the counterpart in the female brain, which explains why sex is always on our mind-quite literally it *is* on our mind. If you were to study, you would find many physiological aspects in the role that the brain plays during sex. But here, I don't intend to engage in that I have relative little knowledge of.

When I suggest that the sex organ between a man's ears is bigger and more important than the sex organ between his legs, I am proposing a deliberate, intentional and creative approach to releasing and indeed exploiting the sexual desires and needs of your spouse, which when done correctly only intensifies the experience for the man. When we introduce mental authority and control into what for many is a mere physical response, so that the entire sexual experience is a wild road trip and not just a destination point, the road will be one that your wife will be eager to travel with you over and over again. The best sex is when two people equally desire and anticipate it, clear their schedules for it and prepare for it knowing that it will be intense and immensely fulfilling for both. If your wife has to be constantly coerced into making love with you, then perhaps you need to humbly find out why. Most women want sex as much as men do, some more!

In an attempt to help us remember some of the points in this chapter I have cleverly assigned them some song titles we all should be fairly familiar with. Don't laugh at the concept-

memorization works best with word association. Of course, there is always the risk that you will never hear these songs again in the same way! Let's get started.

"Oh, That Smell"

Before we can even consider approaching our wives for a little fun, whether planned or spontaneously, our personal hygiene must be checked! Let's clear the air here (another pun intended). I don't care what some sex researchers may try to suggest regarding certain pheromones. Ask any woman about sexual turnoffs, and body odor ranks high as being unsexy. It doesn't matter if you have a long dong like Donkey Kong, if your aroma arrives five seconds before you do, any ambiance you may have hoped to create will be severely dampened if not entirely eliminated.

If our bodies are working properly, we sweat. Sweat itself does not have a bad odor and in fact contains pheromones that can be attractive to mates in certain situations. But the bacteria that quickly grows in dried sweat contains nothing of appeal and offers no benefit to the love-making process. If a quick shower is not in order, a soapy rag or even a disposable wipe can go a long way in turning a stinky proposition into a more acceptable suggestion. This is of even higher importance for couples who enjoy oral sex. Be considerate in this area.

Along with hygiene is bad breath. If your lover can tell you what you last ate, or if your breath can take the curls out of her hair, or if she can become intoxicated just through your intoxication, don't expect a warm reception to your romantic advances. And most certainly do not be offended if she mentions your breath. You should hope you can do the same with her. Oral hygiene is essential the fulfilled experience. The only reasonable exception would be on those days when the two of you wake up in the same mood and start your day with a roll in the hay. Morning breath, though still offensive, can be sacrificed for the morning mood and spontaneous sex while still in the sleepy phase, which makes for one of the most enjoyable of all sexual encounters. At all other times, not so much.

We can't really discuss hygiene without mentioning the hair down there. I will speak candidly about my preferences, lest I make assumptions for a broad base of men that may not be accurate. I personally like a woman to be bare or at the very least neatly trimmed. I believe that the female vagina is beautiful and appealing and I prefer not to have to navigate through the thick of a jungle or get my fingers all tangled up in here in order to find the promised land-that's just my taste (yes, pun intended). Conversely, I might make the similar assumption that women too may not prefer a man whose pubic hairs are so long and dense that they could carry a hair pick in it. While being bare may be a bit extreme for a man, a nice trim every so often just for your wife will make intimacy more enjoyable for her. In fact, if you are so bold and trusting, give her the scissors or trimmer and let her trim away until her heart is content to get the result she prefers. What's the difference anyway, as long as she is pleased. Besides, she may want to play with her newly discovered friend once she can actually see it! Oh, and a penis that is not simply poking his head out from behind the bush, may give the appearance of being larger than one playing hide and seek behind pubes.

Manicures and pedicures are also essential to good sexual hygiene. Nothing says I love you like a gash in your lover's leg due to a jagged toenail. A man's feet will never be sexy, I don't think, but they do need to be clean, odor-free and groomed for safe sex with filed down edges for sexy and enjoyable foot play.

"Your Kiss is on my List"

When I recall my days as a teen and my first dates and first experiences, it wasn't a hand down a blouse that was the first thing to turn me on, it was the kiss! I am a strong advocate of kissing-I truly believe it has become a lost art. I am not referring to that ten second exchange of tongue wrestling some call kissing. No, I am referring to that soul communicating, defenses dropped, hands gently cupping the face, arms around the waist pulling her even closer as if you are trying to literally become one, nothing and no one else exists in the moment, all time stands still, earth-shaking, mountain tremors, tidal waves on the shore, heart exposed, nothing held back, deep, longing, passionate, spiritual, eternal kiss! There is literally nothing more vulnerable or more intimate two people can exchange or share than that kind of a soul exposing kiss. It says I remember the very first kiss, the first time I knew you were the one-every good moment shared in your lives together, every dream and ambition fulfilled, the physical seal of your

126

vows at the onset of matrimony and even for some the last earthly act before that loved one slips away into eternity to await your reunion of souls. There is nothing on earth more loving, more expressive or more fully arousing than that kind of a kiss.

This rare kind of a kiss is one that is not necessarily a prelude to something else, but it *is* the something else. It is that which two people can share for hours and be completely physically fulfilled, that which leaves one feeling incomplete or malnourished when too much time passes from one kiss to the next. It is the sweet taste of love that drips from the corners of your lover's lips which you are compelled to capture in your own lest any should be wasted or lost. No magician of words, no renowned artist, no singer of songs can fully encapsulate the essence of this kind of kiss because words and images don't exist that would come close to doing it justice.

So now you have some glimpse into how much emphasis I place on kissing during intimacy. It is perhaps the best form of foreplay if it leaves her breathless and begging for more. A good kisser can make up for a mound of other inefficiencies in the bedroom, but not everyone has taken the time to even discuss with their partner any kissing preferences or techniques. You may have all the feeling described above, but if your kiss is more like a sink hole waiting for someone to accidentally fall into, then do yourself and her a favor and teach yourself, with her help, how to properly administer the kind of kiss that exposes to her your innermost feelings in a way that excites and stimulates her to be reciprocal in response. Kissing, when done correctly and with the right approach, is not first base, as we were told, but in fact a World Series walk-off Grand Slam!

"Your Body is a Wonderland"

The female anatomy is perhaps the most beautiful of all God's creations, and definitely the most complex. It seems men are trained from puberty that a woman is made up of certain bases with the goal to see how far around the diamond you can get. Unfortunately for some men, their knowledge of a woman's body remains limited to three or four primary parts but not much else.

When I was a boy my father would take us to see our grandparents in Mississippi. It was an eleven-hour drive from our home. Dad's objective was to get there as quickly as possible, making only gas and food stops along the way. I will never forget seeing signs along the highway about certain sights or landmarks and wishing we could take the time to stop along the way and do some exploring, but alas, that was not to be.

Sex should never be approached as a determined destination to the point that you don't stop along the way and do some exploring. The notion that all women are the same and respond similarly to all sexual stimulation is flawed, and if you are just rounding the bases heading for home, you are doing your wife a huge disservice!

Men are funny. They will tear an engine apart just to have a better idea of how it runs and train themselves to diagnose certain noises and symptoms so they know exactly how to make repairs. But when it comes to female anatomy, they either act as if they know everything and can't be taught anymore, or they suddenly become shy teens touching a breast for the first time. And still others may have been raised with strict limitations when it came to sex and when they marry, they are clueless. And sadly, there are those who believe everything they view on a porn site accurately portrays the reality of proper sex technique along with false and unrealistic expectations. They aren't called actors for nothing!

If you fall into any of these categories, or just need a refresher course, there are plenty of sites where you can discreetly research some generalized info such as erogenous (hyper sensitive) zones on a woman's body. But perhaps the best way to learn what makes your lady's engine purr is to tear into it yourself and ask questions along the way. Truth be told, many women are just as shy when it comes to telling their lover what they like and how they like it. But if given the opportunity by your sincere inquiry, they are more than happy to take you on a tour so you can see some of the sights you may have missed in your eagerness to arrive at your final destination.

I will touch briefly on some of the more sensitive areas of her body (yes. Another pun) that most women will share in common. Your job and homework will be to see if your wife shares these zones, and if so to what extent-are some areas more pleasurable than others? Do some areas need to be touched differently? Do some areas have a No trespassing sign posted? The more you learn through mutual and honest communication with your wife, the more pleasure you will be able to provide her and the more fulfilled the two of you will be. Speaking for me, there is little more gratifying than knowing my lover is experiencing orgasmic sensation because of stimulation I am providing. I get off seeing her get off!

The Journey of the Female figure.

Ears. Tracing the outline of the ears can be a super turn on for some women. A gentle nibble or kiss in this area is almost natural since many positions involve being close to her face. Some women may enjoy a light tongue in the ear or maybe light sucking on the lobe. And what woman doesn't love it when their man whispers softly words of love, of passion or even of suggestion into her ears during any intimate act. Good sex is audible, whether a tender and passionate expression or the more primal sounds of heavy mating. They are both seductive and pleasurable and need to be heard. The ear is a part of her body that is engaged in the sexual experience, one way or another. Find out what she likes, and do that!

The Neck. Sometimes underrated, the neck is one of the loveliest parts of a woman. Even ancient Biblical texts describe how beautiful and graceful the female neck can be. The back of the neck, or the nape, covers the top of the spinal column, or nerve central and can be very sensitive and responsive to touch, kisses, massage and even just your warm breath. But the best part of the neck to me is that part that runs from just under her jaw line around to just under her ear. The skin there is smooth and soft to the touch and the slightest stimulus can literally make her hairs stand on end. Whether in bed for the night or sneaking up from behind when she's in the kitchen, attention to her neck will always be well received and appreciated. We all as younger adults and teens heard the term "necking". According to modern terminology, "necking" is the playful caressing of the clothed partner at or above the neck region. Husbands should enjoy necking with their wives.

Breasts. Let us just pause here for a moment and pay proper homage to breasts..
They certainly get our love, respect and attention. And it doesn't really matter if they are big small, A cup or DD-we love them, think about them, envy them and even for the more extreme, worship them, and rightly so. Whether tucked away in a tight-fitting sweater or flaunted through the use of a pushup bra or bikini top, when we see the bumps or the cleavage, we become thirteen-year-old puberty stricken adolescents as if it's still the first time we ever noticed boobs. Whatever your pet name, breasts, tits, boobs, the puppies-we love breasts! But how we love them is extremely important to our ladies. They are not punching bags-they are not handles for better leverage-they are not to be hung on like a swing. They are a special gift that should be treated with care and proper attention and affection.

When many women are ready to be intimate with their partner for the first time, they don't drop the jeans first-they will more than likely remove their shirt or sweater and present their breasts to us. For some it is their indication that now is the time, so women place much emphasis on this part of their body. For most, grabbing the boobs is not a sensual experience. If you listen closely to women who have had sexual experiences with other women, one of the common statements is that women touch each other differently than men touch them. There is a softness, a gentleness, an awareness of the hyper sensitivity surrounding the breasts that sometimes, only other women appreciate. This is why it is so important that you lovingly explore and discuss touch, pressure, technique, etc. with your wife so she doesn't feel like she's being pawed by a grease monkey whenever you touch her. Almost every inch of a woman's breast is sensitive to touch, light caresses, soft kissing-less is often better, as it is with other parts of her body. Sometimes in the heat of making love she will guide your hands to where she wants them to be on her breasts and even guide you in the amount of pressure she wants in any given spot. Pay attention and take mental notes. Some women who are not good or comfortable at discussing things verbally will still tell you all you need to know during the intimate acts themselves.

Some women enjoy having their husband tease her breasts with his penis or slipping it between her breasts and cupping them to form a perfect love tunnel-what guy doesn't enjoy this! Whether it is physically arousing to a woman or just mentally stimulating at the thought of her man's manhood being disappearing into her bosom, this is something you both can take advantage of-often!

And I would be remissed if I did not touch on this very delicate issue. Breast cancer still haunts many women today. With all the breakthroughs in advanced medicine and the treatment of diseases, there is still no known or released cure for breast cancer. For some women the only treatment is a mastectomy, or the removal of one or both of the breasts. I can't adequately put myself in their shoes to express how emotional this must be for some. I would offer this suggestion to men whose wives have battled this horrible

132

disease and endured mastectomies. It is simple really. Treat her exactly the same as if she still had breasts. Spend time and deliberately touch and caress those areas or scars that she hides from everyone else. Let her know that they are beautiful reminders of her fighting spirit and that you couldn't love her anymore. Be aggressive in this so that she knows beyond all doubt that you value her for the light of her love and not the sum of her body parts. This is absolutely not negotiable and the only acceptable response from a loving husband.

Nipples.   Surprisingly to some, men and women experience similar sensations when their nipples are stimulated. That would be because, contrary to some opinions, there are precisely the same number and types of nerve endings in those regions in both male and female. Size of the breast or of the nipple has little to do with response to touch. Because of the thin skin and muscular structure of the nipple, it becomes hard when the nerves are stimulated or exposed to sudden changes like temperature. And the level of sensitivity may be very different from woman to woman, which is why exploration and communication remain so important.

I will speak from my own younger inexperience. I noticed immediately that pretty much any touch was enough for a nipple to become hard, whether aggressive or feather-like. But what I didn't learn quickly (because I didn't ask) was that just because I touched it in a certain way and the nipple responded, I continued the same touch but with increased intensity. I didn't know that the hardening of the nipple was just the beginning of the sexual sensation a woman can experience, even some becoming orgasmic at mere nipple play.

Researchers and studies posted online suggest that the nerves of the nipple send transmitters to the very same erogenous areas of the brain that the vagina or clitoris send, and they bypass the spinal column of nerve central all together, meaning their stimulus is immediately transmitted to the parts of the brain controlling sexual response. We know this to be true as quadriplegics can experience orgasm though paralyzed.

The areola of the breast is that circular pigmented area of skin that circles the nipple. Regardless of the size or color, the areola is also highly charged and super sensitive. If you are paying attention you will usually see that the areola contains mammary bumps that swell when aroused, just like the nipple, so a thorough lover will take all advantage of this sensitivity to maximize his wife's pleasure. Any notion that the nipples are just a temporary stopping point on the way to better things is flawed and you would both be missing out on great pleasure if not enough of proper attention is paid to nipples.

Like breasts, they aren't punching bags or toys but hyper sensitive areas of the body. As always, when stimulating these sensitive areas, less is often more. Hands should be clean and smooth. If you love pleasing your wife, regular use of hand lotion is a plus, especially if you have a job where your hands take a lot of abuse. But don't rely solely on your hands. Sensations can be magnified when certain soft objects are used, like using a real soft feather for the feather-touch effect, or a small piece of silk or satin pulled slowly across the breast. And of course, soft kisses and tongue play is usually always welcomed by your mate as lips have a similar texture and feel as the soft skin of nipples and can be highly arousing. Take your time-stay a while-don't be planning your next move or going through some sort of obligatory exercise with nipples, but rather learn how to use them and enjoy them to your mutual benefit. Her moans of pleasure are a sure indication you need to stay here awhile.

Stomach. Artists during the renaissance days would often highlight the female stomach as it was a sign of fertility and sexuality. Later clothing fashions like halter tops similarly highlighted the sexy belly of a woman. No one wore a halter better or had a sexier belly than Farrah Fawcett in the 70's. Females bellies are plain sexy!

Many people are extremely ticklish in their stomach or rib cage area. This would be again due to the nerves that run through the region. So as with any such region that can be hyper sensitive to touch, the stomach for some women is one of their erogenous zones. It only makes sense as it tends to be a direct highway between the sensitive areas of the breast region and that of the vaginal region, the two more sexually responsive areas of her body. If you are one to go straight from the boobs to the promised land, you have passed over a large area of flesh that can serve to bring your woman to spasms before ever reaching said promised land. Besides, the natural curves of the belly are truly sexy, and certainly a vital entrée of the female buffet. The stomach is a receptor of loving affection.

There is little I enjoyed more than coming up from behind and wrapping my arms around her stomach, and there was little more that she appreciated. The female stomach covers the womb, the place of life! Paying attention and

135

appreciating her stomach tells her you love all that she represents to your life as you wife and as the mother or potential mother of any children the two of you produce. So along with sexual stimulus, there is real emotional attachment assigned to it. Just as with other parts of her body, soft touch, warm kisses, playful licks are all appropriate and welcomed, and if in a position to be kissing her stomach, your hands are free to begin exploring her legs and lower regions, making the sensations ever more heightened. Be a good student and take adequate time with her belly. It's just too good to pass up.

Her Back. I am not sure if even I understand how important the back can be when it comes to both relaxation and foreplay. A person's back is the body's primary core. It contains of course the spinal cord, nerve central, but also certain nerves and a slew of muscles that need to be worked out in all of us from time to time. Many of us hold the stress of the day or the work week in our backs-if our backs hurt, everything hurts! There is nothing better than a good back massage when feeling stiff from work or stressed from the affairs of life. One of the best gifts a man can give his lady is a good back massage. I've done enough of them that I can feel the spots of great tension-it comes not from being smart but from learning about my wife's body and where her pain and stress most likely stem from. This is another thing you can learn a great deal about from online how-to videos coupled with real communication and direction from your wife. As before, smooth hands are essential for maximum pleasure. Lear from practice and repetition how to navigate her back muscles and hot spots so that you are always ready to administer relief. This is one thing she will depend on you for, one thing that, short of an expensive trip a chiropractor

136

or masseur, only you can provide. Exploit it to your advantage by being an expert at it.

Not all massage is for the benefit of a happy ending, at least not immediately. But by being willing to relive the day's tensions from her back upon request, she will be less tired or stressful and who knows where it could lead to, either at the moment or in the near future. And then again, an attentive and completely relaxing massage of her lower back can naturally lead to a southerly direction and perhaps the most attractive part of the female anatomy-God's gift to the brother, the butt!

The Bottom! There are not enough words in the English language, not enough songs or odes to adequately shower praise and adoration on that part that makes men stop dead in their tracks! Some of us have a butt radar-we just know when a sexy female frame is about to be in view. Sir Mix A Lot was right-when *"a girl walks in with an itty-bitty waist and a round thing in your face, you get sprung"* If you can't see the benefit or understand the privilege of spending time on the female bottom at the end of a good massage, you may need more help than this book can offer. I would not be so bold as to suggest that a woman gets much sexual gratification physically from butt play as perhaps with other parts of her body, but surely, she must experience some level of fulfillment knowing she has something that we men absolutely dream about and will do almost anything just to have it in our hands, our belly or our face! After all, if she were to be truthful, she probably has a similar appreciation for ours as well.

It's hard to cover the derriere as a subchapter when so much could be said on the subject. Women use it to get our attention-period. They stuff it in jeans, they allow it to peek out from bikini bottoms, they buy lingerie that highlights the sexy curves, they work it when they walk-all keenly aware that perhaps only a delicious butt arrayed in just the right garment may be the only thing that calls our name more than our favorite sport or must-see game of the week.

Of all the areas of a woman's body she can offer us, the bottom is our just reward for paying proper attention to all other areas of her anatomy-our own Scooby Snack! She will be highly turned on knowing how highly turned on we men get when allowed to play in the backyard. I shouldn't even need to list this as a hot spot on her body!

The butt can be playfully and lightly slapped or grabbed like a lifeline during sex. You need to explore her preferences-she may have many. Her butt can be kissed and nibbled on. The butt can be the preferred access to orally pleasing your wife's genitalia, an access any normal man will spend ample time and attention to. The butt also provides anal access. This is an area that not all women make available, so nothing should be assumed, and yet it's an area that even a liberal female may find difficult in suggesting your attention to. Nothing eliminates false assumptions like communicating about things that are traditionally a taboo subject. Secrets in the bedroom communication are inexcusable.

The Clitoris. The female genitalia, the highly charged super-sensitive little piece of flesh that acts as the "push button to operate" that controls in large part the female orgasm. While men and women have approximately the same number of nerve endings in their respective genital area, that number is greatly concentrated in females into a

138

much smaller area making virtually every touch, every breath, every lick an exaggerated stimulus that done properly can have her singing your name and God's.

Like the male counterpart, the clitoris swells when stimulated or excited and is very responsive to touch. But when and how is critical. Women and their bodies are much more sensitive and need gentle manipulation. You cannot approach the female genitals in the same manner a woman might offer a vigorous hand job for her man. Of course, there will always be exceptions to the rule, that lady who likes to role play or responds sexually to more playful or aggressive methods to achieve her pleasure. It again becomes crucial that you not only experiment but communicate. Men sometimes assume they are doing everything correctly because they hear a woman respond audibly. But a climax can have various levels or stages in females, in addition to being multi-orgasmic, something God left out when he made men.

The sex act isn't necessarily over just because the man ejaculated. If you are quick on the trigger or your wife is eager but a bit slower at reaching the same level of climax, it is imperative, if you want to keep her, to be aware of where she is at in the process, being able to know through experience if she wants more attention and if so, where. There is nothing more frustrating to a woman than for her man to come and strut off beating his chest as if he just did his wife a favor, while she lays there asking if that's the best he's got! Let her be your teacher and by all means be an eager student. The more you know about her sexual profile, how she responds, what she wants and prefers, how long she needs your attention, the more endeared she will be to your future advances.

Learn your way around her clitoris. Don't be afraid to experiment with oils or lotions that increase lubrication. I've heard tell there is nothing more uncomfortable than a man going to town with his dry hands on dry genitals and it will immediately kill the mood. And because this is such a sensitive area and gateway to her entire reproductive system, infections can easily occur if your hands are not thoroughly cleaned before sex. The same goes for your mouth if she enjoys being stimulated orally. The mouth is a host for all manner of germs and bacteria so brush, rinse and be orally disinfected as a loving act for your wife.

Oral stimulation of her clitoris is one of the most pleasurable services you can provide her. I can't recall hearing of any female who finds oral sex distasteful. The thought that her man has willing camped between her legs with nothing in mind but an oral exam of her entire vaginal region alone will send her into spasms. But again, technique and mastery are required. A well-known trick that women applaud is to trace with the tongue the letters of the alphabet. This forcibly provides stimulation from differing angles so that the arousal is exaggerated. Knowing how to trigger her trigger will make her response legitimate, faked. The clitoris is her friend and if you treat it right you will be her BFF (best friend forever).

The emphasis here is that your wife's body is really just one large sex organ, acceptable from many forms of pleasure. Much like a piano only having eight notes in any octave, you can master them to create thousands of beautiful songs-so is your wife's body! The best of lovers will remember the

140

curves and paths that lead to off-road enjoyment in between the peaks and the valley. Enjoy the entirety of your wife's body and appreciate the fact that she is sharing a gift with you and no other, for your mutual pleasure. Don't be in a hurry to touch all the bases with Home Plate being the ultimate prize or she may trade you for a more rounded player with better skills!

"Pour Some Sugar on Me"

One of the most enjoyable and creative ways to keep your sex life from suffering from boredom is to introduce some food into the experience. I am of the opinion that the female body needs very little else in order to be scrumptious. However, some occasions may call for a little play with some sweet delicacies strategically placed or applied that make not only for the world's best dessert, but also for some extra fun stimulation in the consumption of said sugary applications from various parts of her body (and yours!).

I'm sure we've all watched scenes from movies where the Hollywood lover runs an ice cube over his partner's body and watches as she shrieks from a combination of the cold sensation of the ice and the thrill of being simultaneously aroused as it melts into the curves of her flesh. But you don't have to use something as physically shocking as ice. Many food and toppings can offer her the same arousal in more tolerable and playful doses.

Strawberries are a great aphrodisiac that can be shared between two people, if you are using the extra-large and

141

juicy variety. Have your wife take a small bite from the bottom followed by a soft kiss and then proceed to slowly squeeze the juice out to drip wherever area gives her the most pleasure, and then lick it off, slowly but thoroughly-you don't want to leave her sticky as it will ruin the effect. Several other fruits are ideal for this and experimentation is always welcomed.

If you are into Old School music as I am, you may recall an album by The Ohio Players called Sweet Sticky Thing with an image of a beautiful lady with Honey dripping from the jar and into her mouth, one of the sexiest covers of all time. Honey makes for a very tasteful treat for you both so long as it is confined to the smooth parts of her body-no hair. Nothing ruins a mood more than having to take a shower in order to be comfortable, so use honey sparingly but in the same manner you would fruit, slow and deliberate, licking off every last drop.

And then there are the fun toppings like everyone's favorite, whipped cream. Cream in a can may be used to make pictures, shapes, provocative trails that lead from one body part to another, and is a substance that each can take turns with! It's easy to consume and leaves little mess if you are thorough in following the trails.

For the daring there is this thing called edible panties! Yes, they are real. Perhaps a bit expensive considering that the same can be accomplished with anything we've mentioned above, but yet available. Also available, and highly recommended by me, are edible flavored massage oils. They do aid in the massage play much like regular massage lotions would, but unlike other oils, these allow you to kiss or lick parts of the body where the oil has been applied.

142

These oils come in flavors so select one you both agree on as she can use them on you as well.

Play around with different foods to see which ones she most responds to and which bring mutual pleasure. The idea behind food is that you are letting your wife know that you are in no particular hurry and that you view her as a beautiful buffet worthy of your attention to every delicious morsel. Don't assume however that she may enjoy consuming these sweet topping off of you in the same manner. Let her take the lead and decide if and how to relish your anatomy. Honey and chest hair don't go well together. But whipped cream goes with everything!

"I've Been Everywhere"

One of the easiest traps to fall into for couples, especially if there are children in the house, is to relegate sex to the bedroom only. Sometimes the best way to avoid boredom or predictability is to change the scenery. Without giving away too many secrets, I would imagine we could all recall the dating years, especially when we were younger and didn't have our own place, but wanted desperately to be with our girlfriend, how we would make do wherever we could find the opportunity. This is not to advocate premarital sex as that is left up to individual convictions. But the thrill of being sexual in a back seat or in the woods or (fill in the blank) was as exciting as the act itself. So why do we have to resort to using a single designated area for intimacy now that we have both freedom and opportunity?

Spice things up with a change of venue from time to time. If you don't have children in the home, then every room in the house is a possibility. As the book title implies the kitchen is not just for preparing meals. You can make an argument for any number of domestic locations from a cozy sectional to a rug in front of the fireplace to a home office desk to a walk-in shower or even just a sturdy bar stool. Dare I mention a washing machine while it's cycling? You have no idea! And for a little clean fun, who can pass up any opportunity for sex in the shower. The soap makes penetration easy and pleasurable, and self-cleaning! But don't limit your escapades to just the home front.

Sex outdoors in the right atmosphere can be an unbelievable experience. Making love under the moon and stars are the substance of great love songs. You can use a tent, a camper, a sleeping bag or the back of your pickup truck. Be open and honest with each other-ask her for some place she has always dreamed of having sex, and accommodate her. Men, we aren't all physically gifted to the extent that we feel we are doing our wives some favor just by dropping the trousers, but we can all compensate with whatever shortcomings there may be in our game by making sure our mates never get bored with our routine, our position, our timing or a specific sex designated location. If your wife has seen the bedroom ceiling so many times that she has named certain patterns of the ceiling texture, you are slacking in your creativity and limiting if not eliminating any excitement from the sexual experience for her. Variety will keep her interested. So take your love on the road (but take her along for the ride).

144

I can't reiterate enough that predictability, using the same play book over and over, never changing things up, will lead to you and your wife eventually being bored or at least unfulfilled, just as it would if you had meatloaf for dinner every single day. We all love meatloaf, but sometimes we want a steak and sometimes we want a greasy fat-filled cheeseburger or loaded nachos. The same goes for sex. Up to now we have been discussing creative ways to let you woman know you love and appreciate her in every way including sexually, and more times than not, sincere passionate lovemaking is in order. But there will be times when both of you, even if it is never actually discussed, just wants to have sex for the pure physical animalistic response and exchange it is. There's a reason why women want bad boys and some men want a woman "who's a little on the trashy side"-it works both ways usually.

Some may be a bit intimidated at the thought of getting freaky or having sex without all the loving expressions, especially if raised in conservative environments. But I am of the conviction that anything is acceptable between two consenting committed marriage partners who have no objections. All guards should be dropped between two lovers who want a long lasting non-boring love life and men need to find their comfort zone and then bust right through it. Artists have made millions off songs that deal with the rawness of sex, but loving and diving head first into the purity of intercourse is not exclusive to secular song fans. Many marriages could be spared, and affairs decreased if couples would simply enjoy times where all the rules were thrown out and you just did whatever comes naturally to the mutual pleasure of both man and woman.

Be verbal on these occasions, and don't be bashful. Play a role if you have to but make it enjoyable for her. Feel free to tell her things like, what a nice ass she has or how you love her tits or what you want to do to her. Dirty talk between lovers will certainly spice things up, especially if she is not accustomed to hearing you speak that way. Don't overdo it but be bold, be blatant and be direct. Monitor her response if it is your first few times and discuss it after to see if she was just accommodating you or if it was a turn on for her. Not all women are the same so generalizations can't always be applied here but communication will eliminate any false assumptions. And this leads to the next song.

"Good Vibrations"

I must admit when the subject of adult toys being introduced to make things more interesting, at first, I was a bit offended. The ego in me, and I might presume many men, kicked in, something to the tune that I should be all she needs. How backward thinking and archaic that conclusion. Instead I should have been grateful that my partner was open enough to suggest it. Had I been more informed and less egotistical, I would have suggested we meet at a local Adult Toy Store where she could pick out that which she envisioned, even if it was a reasonable facsimile that I may not measure up to. Us of the more conservative background need to be more open to the use of mechanical devices and understand that they don't replace us, they merely aid in our wife experiencing prolonged or multiple orgasms of which we are in control of. This is especially true of men who in spite of their best efforts are a bit quick on

146

the draw. We should never be alarmed or take offense if the wife brings up the topic of adult toys for the enhancement of her sexual experience. In fact, knowing what I do now, I believe a conscientious husband will be the first to ask his wife if she would enjoy having such aids at their disposal.

Vibrators come in a wide variety of shapes and sizes depending on the intended use. Most who think of vibrators probably picture dildos, or penis lookalikes made for vaginal penetration. But many are much smaller and not intended for insertion but just for stimulation. The can be very discreet and unassuming but deliver a vibrating sensation that no normal male could ever produce. These artificial mechanical stimulations can drive a woman insanely wild when used correctly. Therefore, in addition to being open for their use, men must be open to be properly trained on how and where to best apply them to make their lover scream.

There are also fingertip varieties, very small in size but attachable to the fingers so that your normal slow caress of her body is now done so with an invigorating and chilling charge that she will love and respond to openly and audibly, which can be a huge turn on for men. There should be nothing more arousing to a man than to know that at his touch or control, he is sending his wife into physical spasms of sensual pleasure. It should be as fulfilling as ejaculating.

An open and willing attitude regarding the use of sex toys in a marriage can be a game changer, one in which you always come out a winner in your wife's eyes.

The perfect song to discuss sexual positions, a couple of which being Cowgirl positions. Savvy lovers know that there are more positions for making love than just the old-fashioned man-on-top missionary position. Experimenting with various positions offers so many benefits for all kinds of reasons. Some positions clearly put the man in charge while other let the wives take the lead. Some positions are better for freeing up our hands to explore her body while others require us to hold on for leverage. They allow for different views of her body, they allow you to lay back and enjoy watching her respond to you, and on and on.

But there can also be strategic reasons why women may prefer one position over another. Not all men are eight to ten inches long, so some position may provide deeper penetration for those challenged by length. Some positions may provide more direct stimulation of certain vaginal regions than others. The idea here is that there is more than one way to skin a cat (these puns are just too easy). Discuss and experiment with them. Here are some of the more popular positions.

Missionary

The tried and true baby-maker position, woman on bottom with legs spread and the man on top. It's simple, easy, and most likely the first position most engage in, and sadly, the only one others use. This position may provide the most intimacy as it places lovers directly across from each other for eye contact and kissing.

148

Doggy Style

The "Who Let the Dogs Out" style preferred by many men. Most men love this position as it provides the best for rear or backdoor entry, but it also provides an amazing view of your wife's beautiful ass, a natural turn-on for most men. This position also plays to the animalistic instinct common to most men as a raw sexual response. Playful slaps on the butt are also a benefit. But more important, it can provide better stimulation of a woman's G-spot, the bumpy ridge on the top of her vaginal wall that has its own orgasm named after it because it's so intense. Other positions will aid in G-spot orgasms as well.

69

For lovers of oral sex and stimulation, there is no better way or mutually beneficial position than the 69 position. As the actual number "69" implies, the head-to-foot positions are reversed, usually with the woman on top, but also each on their side, so that her vagina is within easy oral access to her man's face and she is face-to-face with his other head. This is not usually a position for the long haul because the pleasure is so electrifying that is won't take long for each to experience orgasm. It is not, however, conducive to communication as besides being at opposite ends of each other, it's hard to talk with your mouth full.

Spooning

Spooning is a position for intimacy. As the term implies, the couple lie on their sides, man behind the woman so that penetration is from the rear but hands are free to caress. It's another great G-spot position for the woman. In addition to being a great position for sex, it's also a very natural and comfortable position to simply fall into a deep and blissful sleep immediately after both are left breathless.

The Speed Bump

I lik-ee this position very mucho! There is nothing more arousing than the feel of your woman's butt pressed against your stomach! This is a position where the woman lies flat on her stomach, legs together and the man lies on top of her and enters her from behind. Because it's such a turn on for most men, it again may not be a position for the long haul, but it is the only speed bump a man will actually slow down for and go over slowly, and if like me, back up and go over again and again.

The Cowgirl

A great position for G-spot orgasms. It's also great for a man because he gets to simply lie back and watch his beautiful sexy wife. In this position the man is flat on his back and the wife straddles him in a sitting position facing toward him, her hands on his chest for leverage. She is free to ride and control both the tempo and the depth of the thrusts she wants in order to achieve climax. She is in complete control in that instance as to how long each of you will last. And the man gets to lay back and take it all in.

Reverse Cowgirl

This position is the same as above but with the girl facing toward the man's feet, her hands on his legs. Again, a great way for her to control the action and for the man to enjoy a different perspective of his woman controlling the action from the best view, the rear!

The Face Off

This is one of the more intimate positions for long and loving sessions. The man will sit on a chair or the edge of the bed and the woman will sit on his lap facing him and wrapping her arms and legs around him. Once she is in position and with the penis inside her it's just a loving face-to-face experience that can go on for a long time. Once she is getting close, however, the man is free to grab her butt and help in the thrusting speed or penetration depth until both are pleasantly exhausted.

The Anvil

A variation of the Missionary, it involves the woman on her back but bringing her legs or calves over the man's shoulders. This allows for deep penetration and is great for men not heavily endowed. It also directly stimulates the G-spot. This position is fine for bed but can be easily used on harder and elevated surfaces like a table or counter

Kitchen Confidential

Sex begins in the kitchen, but sometimes it can end there as well. A kitchen counter or table will do. The woman sits on the counter facing you, and the man stands in front of her while she wraps her legs around him. This is a great position for couple who enjoy watching the thrusting and provide deep penetration, and quick access to an after-sex snack. Just be sure to have your wife slightly over the edge or the only snack you will be having is cracked nuts!

151

The L or the T

Not as common but just as pleasurable, this position offers variety for the more flexible. The woman is on her back, perpendicular to her man who is on his side facing her. Her legs go over his hip as he penetrates her semi-from behind. The position resembles the letter "L" or "T". Performed correctly and she'll be reciting all kinds of letters before you are finished.

OK, so I've rattled off an even-dozen different positions you can experiment with. Not all positions are for everybody, and I certainly left many off the list. Not all positions involve penal penetration but are instead just for oral or hands-free stimulation. There is nothing new under the sun, and body styles, flexibility, physical impairment will all factor into which positions may be both pleasurable and comfortable for both parties, but half the fun is the discovery process of experimentation, so be daring and open to your mutual enjoyment and fulfillment.

"Girls Just Want to Have Fun"

Most of this chapter has intentionally addressed how the husband should love, handle, stimulate and fulfill his wife. It's just a normal perception that men are givers of pleasure and women are the receivers. But that may not be the case every time. Some women may actually get their pleasure by giving men theirs. There is nothing sexier than when a woman pushes her man back into bed and takes over. ALL MEN should be open and grateful for a woman like that!

Today's modern fashion for men isn't what it used to be, although in many southern states it hasn't changed. Ask a young woman what she likes best when looking at a man and she most likely will respond just like we would-a nice butt in a pair of tight Wrangler or Levis. I can't tell you how hard it is to find jeans for men anymore that aren't "relaxed" or loose fitting. If women wore jeans the way men do there would be much less temptation because today's men's fashion is anything but sexy, except maybe to those women who are just as turned on by a nice suit and tie.

Just like men, many women thoroughly enjoy orally pleasing their man or working him into a lather with her hands. If you are blessed to be married to a lady who enjoys doing you as much as you enjoy doing her, drop to your knees and thank God above! You hit the jackpot and keeping things interesting in your bedroom, or wherever, will be much less challenging. Be open to fulfilling your wife's fantasies if she wants your body that badly. While we men may not have nearly the erogenous zones a woman has, if it turns her on, let her go for it. Be willing, against all that may seem natural to you, to be the recipient of her touch, whether she wants your penis, wants to lick your nipples or even play with your butt-yeah, I know, but hey, if she's happy, she will make us happy. Never say never in the bedroom. Let your girl have her fun.

"Hot for Teacher"

I can imagine all of us men at one time or another in our school years had the hots for one of our teachers that filled our heads (both heads) in our dreams. This song has much to do with role playing. Admittedly, it's a subject that gets mixed reviews from marriage counselors. Innocent role playing can be enjoyable if it is mutually agreed to and if it spices up an otherwise mundane sex life. Roles can vary from student/teachers to cop/prisoner to boss/employee and others I'm sure. Dressing up and playing a role for mutual gratification in and of itself should not be viewed as twisted, just unusual.

However, role playing can be detrimental in certain situations. If the roles you desire involve anything that would in normal circumstances be deemed illegal, i.e. statutory, incest, rape, etc., then one really needs to examine the fixation on such roles as they may indicate issues that need to be addressed through therapy-no joke.

Another detriment to role playing is escaping reality. For example, if the only way you can enjoy sex with your wife is for her to pretend to be something or someone she isn't, this is aa bad sign that something is severely broken in your relationship and no amount of role playing will ever change things. If a role is preferred because you simply don't love your wife as she is, then counseling is in order if you wish to save your marriage.

So in summary, I have attempted to discuss things in this chapter involving the beauty of the sexual experience between two committed people, a subject often left unmentioned with some counselors and certainly most churches. Loving your wife in all things and in all ways, especially sexually, should not be a subject we are afraid or too intimidated to approach, regardless of our upbringing or our comfort level. Man and woman were created by a unique God with unique needs to give and receive pleasure-nothing has changed from then up to now except maybe an openness to discuss what traditionally has been left behind closed doors. But the idea I tried to relay is that if you take these ideas or techniques, play with and discuss them with your wife, tweak them to be more individual to her exact needs, you can create a loving, exciting, never boring love life that will allow you to be her ever-changing lover for years to come. An old saying goes something like, the best lover isn't one who has loved a thousand women, but rather one who has loved one woman for a thousand years. I wish I'd come up with that because it's pure and profound. Don't become another statistic because you failed to actively engage in proper training, experimentation and communication when it comes to satisfying and pleasuring your wife. Worship the gift of her body-cherish the beauty of her sexuality-explore the depths of her desires and fill every crevice of her innermost fantasies. Make her want you and you alone-give her no cause to consider anyone else-take nothing for granted and recognize bedroom boredom for the cancer it is to a marriage, the remedy being excitement, variety, spontaneity and exploration. In this way you will eliminate one of the leading causes of today's divorce.

16. If You Are Looking for Bathsheba, You Will Find Her

In scripture there is a story of a man named David, the King of Israel. King David had everything any man could ever want. He had power and authority as the nation's ruler, he had fame and riches from his many battle victories and the resulting plunder, he was a gifted musician that others loved to hear, and he had the most beautiful women in all of Israel as his wives. He literally had it all. Everything except one woman.

One night while strolling the roof of his palace, he spotted a woman in another dwelling bathing and he was immediately struck and captured by her beauty. He could have simply admired her as we all would, and moved on. But instead, he stayed, he gazed, and he became fixated on her. He obsessed over her-dwelled on her-fantasized over her until the burning desire was too great to deny, so he, being King, sent for her and took her for his own, even though she was married to another man, one of the King's own Army officers. It was a lack of discretion that would eventually cost him dearly.

In today's world it isn't very difficult for a man to come across beautiful women he may find irresistible, having a sexual attraction perhaps greater than that for his own wife. Being attracted to other women or appreciating the beauty and physical features of another woman is natural and usually not a problem. Even women will notice and sometimes comment on other women. It is not in the noticing where trouble begins, it's in the obsession, the refusal or inability to see, appreciate and move on that allows obsession to give birth to temptation which gives birth to infidelity. There is little more unforgivable than for a man to become unfaithful to a wife who has given him absolutely no reason to stray-he just saw something he had to have and couldn't help himself. In most cases, the thrill of the affair is not worth the price paid through a broken relationship, a broken family and divorce.

I've heard both men and women make comments along the line that chasing other women is just something that men do-it's in their genes (or jeans as, more accurately). I find this excuse to justify and defend infidelity and unfaithful husbands reprehensible. You have this beautiful woman who has committed her life to being your companion, perhaps given you children, offered her body to you alone, tolerated your bad days and struggles, many times without notice or thanks, and finds honor in being your wife. But you so easily dismiss all of that when a tight ass or cleavage captures your attention in a flattering manner and you feel that youthful need for conquest. In that moment of weakness your wife, your children, their futures and welfare are all discarded so you can have a physical encounter to satisfy a temporary urge, just like King David, and the results of a moment of pleasure are a broken home, a broken trust and a divided family with visitation rights on weekends.

No marriage is perfect. If you successfully implement everything in this book, there will still be missteps, bad days, quarrels and challenges that just naturally happen when two people share lives every day. If a man is looking for some superficial excuse to wonder into the arms of another woman, it will be easy enough for him to find one and justify it in his own mind. "She's not the same woman I married" or "she just doesn't understand me anymore" or "she doesn't meet my physical needs". There exists the theory of the seven-year itch that implies that after a matter of years of being together men just by nature begin to look for someone new because they get bored easily and need some excitement. Truth be known this happens with women as well. The whole idea behind the composition of this book is to find and implement ways to prevent boredom and monotony so that these false indicators of needing something new and fresh do not overwhelm a man's ability to reason with his larger head and make the better decision for his marriage and his family.

Let's be honest men. Unless you look like George Clooney we still need and seek affirmation from other women. We want to know we still have some appeal to the opposite sex, other than our wives. We want to know if we still have it and could attract someone else if we wanted to. We want to know if younger more youthful women find us sexy as older men. This is why innocent flirtations become gateways to unfaithfulness and casual soliciting glances become a night in a hotel room. For some reason, many men discount the every-day affirmation they receive from their own wives and

158

find more weight and value in the approval of women they come in contact with through extracurricular activities outside of the home. Even a man with the strongest of resolve can become a victim to the temptation of a pretty young thing who makes us an offer we simply can't or won't refuse. King David was a happy man and didn't know he wanted anything more until he saw his Bathsheba and knew that he could have her if he wanted her badly enough. All men have their Bathshebas.

Our Bathshebas may be women we work with, the young secretary or the woman who shares an office or cubicle with us. Workplace affairs are so common and predictable for a very good reason. We spend the best and most productive eight hours of every day, not with our wives but with our coworkers. We may have our morning coffee with them, we take our lunch breaks with them, we spend meetings with them and in some cases, are required to travel with them. That's a full eight hours each day. Compare that with the time spent at home with your wife. You may see each other for an hour over breakfast in a sleepy haze before rushing off to work. You return at the end of the day for 4-5 hours exhausted from the day's activities and are off to bed, to sleep. So, as you can see, not only does your wife get fewer hours with you than your job does, she gets the hours when you may not be at your best. She may be giving you all the attention you could ever want but you are too tired to see it, but you instead see that your coworker gives you much wanted attention and you receive it better because you are in your more productive and alert hours. It's a vicious cycle.

Men must recognize this phenomenon for what it is and deal with it proactively in your reasoning and deliberately in your actions. Avoid excess time spent with coworkers that the job doesn't require. Remind yourself of the loving family you are working hard to support. Recall precious moments spent with your wife that will vanish into thin air like a mist that never existed if you follow through with sexual urges for another woman. Guard your heart against intruders like you are guarding your home against would-be burglars.

There are certainly other opportunities for a man to spot his Bathsheba. You want your wife to continue to be physically attracted to you, so you go to the gym to work out three or four nights per week. Gyms can by a disaster for a man wanting to remain faithful. There you see women who are not only beautiful and physically fit, but you see them in some of the most revealing workout clothes imaginable. From shorts to yoga pants, there is little left to imagine, and her form is on display for anyone who wants to notice. You make a connection because you are both physically active and share common fitness goals. You become workout buddies which not only allows you to spend time with her, but puts you in even closer proximity to her body which captured your attention in the first place. You watch each other sweat, share a juice at the juice bar afterwards and it just happens. You didn't see the warning signs, or you ignored them because she flattered you with her attention and you didn't put up any resistance. The end result is the same, a momentary discretion causes a lifetime of regrets.

Think you are above all that because you are a good church-attending husband? Guess again. Because people in a church feel they are protected by a shared faith, they mistakenly drop their defenses. An innocent cup of coffee after a service or a ride home because it's on the way, and oops, you did it again. This Bathsheba is the most deceitful of all because she comes to you at the very place you seek strength and guidance to avoid such advances and men are completely caught off guard.

You see, it doesn't really matter where you are, where you spend time, how strong you think you are in your marriage, there are Bathshebas waiting for men around every corner. There are the ones you are actively looking for because of some perceived inadequacy in your marriage, and there are the ones who are actively seeking a safe night of passion and a married man tells no secrets. It's almost like walking through a firing range training session where the enemy can literally pop up anywhere and at any time and you have to be ready to defend yourself and your marriage against any and all attacks. But this can only be possible when a man is truly 100% committed to his marriage. As soon as any doubt creeps in, any feeling of being unappealing to your wife, any hint of getting old, you open the door just enough for the slightest shadow of compromise to enter.

Again, if you haven't been in a long-term relationship that failed, you can't know how devastating it is to be looking in on family activities like a poor child peering into the window of a department store he can't enter. It is heartbreaking and gut-wrenching and leaves you with haunting regrets and constant reminders that you alone are responsible for your marital demise. Know how to spot a Bathsheba in your life. Identify in your mind women you may already know who might be the one, activities you engage in where they may be revealed and reasons why you would take notice in the first place. Work now while you can to eliminate any and all occasions where time spent in compromising situations would lead to any lack of sane judgment. If an alcoholic knows he can't say no to liquor, he knows to stay out of bars or anyplace where liquor is being served. In the same manner, learn how to avoid opportunities where your resolve would be tested and lead you to fall off of the marital fidelity wagon.

17. Conclusion

Marriage unfortunately doesn't come with an instruction manual. If so, it would have to be a manual unique to each couple in consideration of the numerous qualities and traits that make us all individual, and unique couples. However, I have attempted to compile a guide based on similarities we all share, desires we are all born with and just a little hard-knocks advice from someone who has had a few successes in relationships, as well as a few very unfortunate failures. I have at no time claimed to be an expert in any marriage related field of study, and I confessed upon my introduction that I possess neither credentials nor degrees nor anything that would cause others to seek me out for advice on a professional level. With that disclosure, it is my intent to present this with all the sincerity and humility possible as a lay-person who simply wants to share my experiences, in an effort to help other men from going down the path of pride or ignorance I traveled at the high cost of my long-term marriage.

Having made this disclosure, I truly feel that if such a real and vulnerable book like this one had been made available to me many years ago, with strategies spelled out in easy-to-understand terms, with methods I could have easily applied in my marriage, I and my family may have been spared a world of heartache and pain, and the consequences of failed marriages and split families. Bare-naked advice like this doesn't normally get handed down from generation to generation. Nor is it offered in today's churches. Older couples stay married just because that's the way they were taught, happy or not, while younger couples have been conditioned to believe that if the relationship isn't working it's much easier and accepted to simply end it by decree of divorce rather to fight for it and work it out. Christians often will say that God hates divorce, as a form of some sort of condemnation, to guilt couples into staying together. I am completely convinced that God does hate divorce, but only because in His sovereignty He is aware of the hurt and the pain, and even guilt the couple will endure, as well as the emotional implications of a family divided.

In some ways I wish the local church would take more of an active role in training and mentoring couples in and during marital issues, and not just be finger pointers after the fact. God created sex-let's talk about it! God created romantic, *eros,* love-let's discuss it. Let's have sponsored training and private seminars to discuss how best to please our spouse and cement our relationships, and how to endure the storms that come against any relationship with time. Let's be more open, more frank, more honest about our fears, our hurts and disappointments so that remedies can be reviewed and practiced, instead of simply keeping the resentments bottled up until the love has been put to sleep. Let's be more explicit in sexual techniques and proactive as mentors unashamed, in lieu of learning incorrectly from false media and websites. Let's be as brazenly passionate about our marriage as we are about political ideals. It's amazing to me how easily and eagerly we can take up a political or social cause, march, protest, voice strong opposing ideas without any fear or intimidation, but clam up when it comes to the much more important issues of our marriages. There should be no guilt or shame in admitting a less than perfect relationship. The guilt and shame should come only after you allowed pride and ignorance to keep you from taking all measure to fix the problems before they became terminal... much like I did.

Marital love and all its beauty should be desired, treasured and protected, especially by us men. There is a story in the scriptures of a farmer who one day found a rare and priceless gem in his field. So the farmer, realizing its worth, went and sold all his land and possessions just to acquire this one special gem. The lesson is that when you find such a love with your mate, it should be viewed as the priceless gem that it is, and should be cherished, desired and protected at all cost. This approach to marriage will manifest itself in attitude and awareness, resulting in a relationship other couples will be envious of, and one your children will want to emulate!

By the time this book is published I will have been divorced for eight to nine months. I may no longer be in the mourning process but there is not a day that goes by that I don't think about my former wife, and run through the mental list of regrets I carry over the role I played in allowing our marriage to end. As I spend lonely hours at night viewing old photos of happier times, remembering each occasion, I am visited by ghosts that torment me. For some, divorce may be the freedom they are longing for. For me, it is a haunting that is fitting for a cold October night. As I mentioned in my introduction, it is not something I would wish on my worst enemy, and if there is anything I can do to prevent it from happening again, or to help other men to take measures now to prevent the same fate, this effort will have been worth it.

There is nothing more beautiful in the entire universe than new love, the freshness and excitement of discovery when two people come together to create a new life for themselves. There is no rule or standard written or expressed to suggest this newness has to end. We use the common phrase; *the honeymoon is over.* But why does it have to be over? Who says couples can't still be giddy with each other after a year, five years, ten years or longer? We have been conditioned to accept things as normal, but normalcy is not always a good or productive thing! We shouldn't necessarily be able to look at a couple's countenance and determine how long they've been married by their scowls. Nor should we assume that if a couple can't keep their hands off each other that they must be newlyweds! Our perception and conditioning in regard to relationships is flawed and couples who want something more, should feel free to recast the marriage mold. I know for sure that if I ever take the chance again, it will only be with someone who shares the ideals of love, of laughter, of adolescent behavior that will keep a relationship from ever getting stale, monotonous or common. I only wish I had adopted this resolve much earlier.

I reside in Las Vegas. I love playing live poker. Poker can be played from a very conservative position, that is protecting what you have in your hand but not being willing to bet out because you aren't convinced your hand will hold up. Or, it can be played from a very aggressive position, that is betting in each round regardless of how convinced you are of your hand, and ultimately going all in with confidence of your winning hand.   Marriage should always be an all-in proposition, none of this fifty-fifty crap.   Men, if you love your wives, if you want her affection, if you want sex and intimacy to continue to be thrilling for you both, if you never want to grow tired of her or your marriage, you need to play all-in every day.   Do you want another analogy men can relate to? When an NFL team gets a lead and then starts to play to simply to protect their lead, that is, to play not to lose, they usually lose. When you go from the offensive strategy to the defensive, the game doesn't usually end well. You have to play to win. Your marriage is your Super Bowl.

We have discussed in great detail some ways and methods you can incorporate into your relationship to keep the fires burning and the youth of love intact. How you choose to handle and apply these instructions are now up to you.   If you are reading this book, it is most likely not too late, but you need to determine right now what you want from your marriage and how hard you are willing to work to make that happen.

If there were some magical spell I could cast that would create within you a passion for your marriage I would certainly employ such a spell over everyone who reads these words.   But only you can create or resurrect that magic in your marriage.   At one time she was the spark in your eye and the smirk in your smile and the strut in your walk.   She can be again. There is nothing to prevent it except your own inhibitions or foolish stubbornness or some false man code that disallows vulnerability.   Pride is a cancerous evil. Admitting you might be wrong about something or that perhaps there are things you could learn seems foreign to many men.   While women may admire strength and conviction, they are equally drawn to a willingness to be humble and gentle. If this is what is needed to save a marriage or to recreate the newness that has been lost, then humble and gentle and vulnerable men should be!

Believe me when I tell you there is little worse than being right, but being alone. A woman definitely brings her share of issues into a relationship as no one is perfect in all things, but the response of a husband should be one of a willingness at all costs to see the lady he married as his forever bride and to strive, as much as it is within his ability, to be the best, the most loving, the most passionate and affectionate man he can be to his bride so that when storms come along, and they will, they are met quickly with a mutual resolve to weather them together and move on. A couple's ability to successfully navigate life's challenges is a true indicator of the strength of the marriage. In so many ways, as I have attempted to point out, this strength relies on the man and his approach to the relationship.

From the beginning institution of marriage couples have had issues, disagreements and fights. If a man was to successfully employ everything we have discussed in this short book, there will still be arguments and differences of opinions and philosophies when it comes to marriage and families. But if there are things that you as the husband can do to reduce these challenges, or to better identify them so you can quickly address them to preserve peace and joy in your relationship, wouldn't you apply them all? The strongest of men or company executives can be brought down by an unhappy wife or marriage. I learned much too late that it doesn't need to be this way. This may not be the end-all book on marital conflict, but it is my hope that some simple soul-searching and a refocused perspective on the purpose of your relationship by applications of the topics we covered, will enhance, renew or serve as a guide and manual for men who truly desire the best possible and fulfilling marriage with their wives. If but one marriage is saved, one heartache like mine avoided, or one family unit prevented from the emotional scars of divorce, I can die knowing I left a little something positive behind that I can be proud of. God bless every person who reads this book with the marriage they always dreamed of. It can happen!

Made in the USA
Monee, IL
28 November 2019